AF245592

Cover design by Graeme Cogdell.
Illustrations by Greg Haar.

First printing December 1985

National Library of Australia
Cataloguing-in-Publication data

Krause, Jonathan, 1959-
   I love a sunburnt stomach.

   ISBN 0 85910 378 1.

   1. Meditations   I. Title.

242'.63

Printed and published by
Lutheran Publishing House,
205 Halifax Street, Adelaide, South Australia.

I Love a Sunburnt
Sunburnt
Stomach

Jonathan Krause

Lutheran Publishing House, Adelaide

for
Mum and Dad

and
in memory of
my grandparents,
who gave me
a history

My grandparents and me, on the day of
my baptism — August 2, 1959.

What You Get

I Was
ere
Krause

Before

G'day!

The thing you're holding in your hands is the end-result of about 400 hours of my crummy two-fingered typing, and about 25 years of my flitting around this rock we human beings call home.

There are a few reasons why I wrote this book. The most important, I guess, is that I'm a Christian, who wants to share what he knows about God with others. A book seemed a good way for me to do it — it's a bit harder to get shy and tongue-tied when you're safe between two covers.

I hope you haven't read a book like this before. Most of the books about God that I've read have been rather heavy, and some have been downright crushing. I've tried to lighten the load a bit here. I hope that the stories will be interesting, that maybe you'll laugh a few times, and that sometimes you'll stop to think. Jesus was a brilliant communicator — he had the crowds hanging on every word he spoke — and in my clumsy way I've tried to follow his lead.

I reckon God wants us to do what we can do. I like writing, so here's a book.

Maybe some of you would prefer that any Christian message here be wrapped up in a couple of short sentences — so you could get through it quickly, or just skip right over the top. And I must admit that I don't go for the sledge-hammer approach to evangelism, either. Sometimes, though, we have to work through stuff that is just straight teaching, and I don't apologize for where that happens here. I just ask that you hang in there.

If, when reading this book, you catch me saying that you 'should' do something, you have my permission to stop reading and to call me a knucklehead. I don't want to tell anyone what they 'should' do; I just want to share what I think is the best thing to do. So, I'd appreciate it if you could interpret it that way every time you come across the word 'should'.

After you've read this book, I hope you'll be inspired and curious enough to go to its source, the Bible. That's where you'll get the first-hand, direct-from-God information.

In case you want to know a bit about the person telling these stories, I'll give you some biographical details. If you don't want to know, skip the next paragraph.

I'm 25 years old, and pushing middle age. I've been married a couple of years to a cutey little blonde called Kanny. Her real name is Karen, but I only call her that when I'm mad with her, so I won't use it here. I'm working toward a Bachelor of Arts degree, with which I hope to be able to get some sort of job — even taxi driving. I've always enjoyed writing, and a couple of years ago had a book published called *for a friend* . . . I write a bit of poetry, and some fairly weird short stories, and then things like those in this book. And . . . that's enough about me — I can see you yawning.

I hope you enjoy reading this, and I hope you can hear God talking to you between the lines. That's my prayer, anyway.

Marathon man

Marathon man — not the Dustin-Hoffman-movie-type marathon man, but the Robert-de-Castella-puffing-over the-finish-line-type.

Ahh, the sweat, the energy, the glory of it all! The power that pumps legs of iron, kilometre after kilometre, hour after hour, until that final marvellous moment: the victorious entry into the colosseum, the lap of glory, the plaudits of the huge flag-waving crowd, and the ABC's Norman May shouting: 'GOLD! GOLD! GOLD!'

It's inspiring, isn't it?

I nearly *expired* from the massive dose of inspiration the 1984 Olympic marathon set in me. It put me on an athletic high that I was unable to control. I undertook my own marathon — a jog to the letterbox and back, a distance of at least twenty metres, including *three* steps!

After that massive effort, thoroughly exhausted, and with chest heaving, heart pounding, face red, and eyes bulging, I had to sit down. The only compensation for the pain I endured was that my enforced rest gave me time to reflect on a few previous examples of my sporting prowess. (I actually reflected on only one example, but I am so unfit that it felt like many).

Unfortunately, I have never been a brilliant competitive athlete. Let me quickly add that this is no fault of my own. It appears that I was created with under-sized lungs, over-sized belly, and legs that are at least fifteen centimetres too short. This is not to mention the fact that someone had a real joke on me, putting pimples where muscles were supposed to be. These are all due to genetic factors, and can in no way be attributed to any laziness on my part, or my fondness for a particular brand of chocolate bar —creamy, golden, luscious, and richly smothered in thick milk chocolate.

However, despite being inherently unathletic, I have sometimes been forced to compete. You know what it's like at school sports days — they always seem to be one sucker short for the long-distance events: the 47 kilometre uphill sprint, the cross-mud-country swim, and so on. I always tried to be somewhere else when the race was on, but somehow I always seemed to be found just in time and dragged screaming to the starting line.

There are some people — a very strange breed that I can in no way understand — who, although not athletically gifted, *do* still try very hard. They pant and sweat and strain and train and make a real effort. They are the sort who throw up after a race, and require massive doses of pure oxygen before they can be resurrected from the timekeeper's table on to which they've crashed. I am *not* one of those sort of people, and I suspect I've got a few mates out there, especially if I mention cross-countries, for example.

I am very scientifically minded when it comes to expending some of my store of energy. I understood from Maths classes that the shortest distance between two points was a straight line, so I could not work out why the designers of cross-country courses deviated so far from this principle. The only way to cope with this was to *rearrange* their course, to rationalize it, make it more efficient, literally cut corners.

Now, as with all great scientific endeavours, there are bound to be some risks and some unforeseen side-effects. With regard to cross-countries, under these categories can be included starving German shepherds, electric fences (which add a whole new zing to the sport of hurdling), giant cowpats, enraged property-owners, and prowling, sharp-eyed, cross-country-course marshals.

Yes, the risks were great, but so too were the rewards. Nothing as egotistical as winning, but merely survival. The consummate pleasure of still being able to breathe, and perhaps to have enough energy to half-strut around the finishing line, impressing the ladies, without bursting more than two or three of the more important blood vessels leading to and from the heart.

And so, there it is: my reflections on my sporting prowess, my athletic achievements, my short-cuts to success. If only life — and, in particular, Christian life — were that simple. St Paul talks about a Christian being like an athlete:

'Surely you know that many runners take part in a race, but only one of them wins the prize. Run, then, in such a way as to win the prize. Every athlete in training submits to strict discipline, in order to be crowned with a wreath that will not last; but we do it for one that will last for ever' (1 Cor. 9:24,25).

You see, the thing about being a Christian, trying to live as Christ lived, is that there are no short-cuts. It's just plain hard work. It's a matter of sweat and energy and persistence and disappointments and hurting. It takes discipline.

An athlete in training keeps away from junky foods, even the wonderful things in life like Big Macs and triple-strength chocolate milkshakes. No matter how much the athlete loves those things, he or she stays away from them. Like athletes, Christians have to keep away from the things that are going to drag down their performance, even if those things seem to be the most delicious and most tempting things in the whole world.

An athlete trains for an event: runs laps, does exercises, practises times. The Christian trains too: by reading God's Word, praying, worshipping, helping and serving others.

Training, by its very nature and purpose, is not easy. It gets boring, and requires too much time and too much effort, and it may be that sometimes we feel like we just can't be bothered any more. That's when we require self-discipline and, just as importantly, encouragement; we need the encouragement God gives us through our fellow-Christians, the inspiration to hang in there, to keep on going.

And why all this training and effort?

Not to win the victory of Paradise by our own efforts — for that's impossible — but to respond to Christ's winning the victory for us — the victory over sin and death and the power of the devil.

I never expect to catch up to Christ in my life here on earth, but I'm in training so that I can be as close to him as possible. I'm hanging in there, working as hard as I can, looking forward to the victory celebration in heaven. GOLD! GOLD! GOLD!

Jimmy Watson and me

The waiter was slim, blue-eyed, and French. His name was Christian, and he had the sort of accent that Australian girls collapse in ecstasy at. 'Vood you like your vine ohpen, sir?'

'Nah, I just brung it to look at. Course I want it open, you Frog fritter!'

Christian eased the cork from the bottle. After a gentle struggle, it succumbed with that pure crisp popping sound unique to well-corked Cabernets, almost the sound of a delicate 'Egad'.

I sniffed the cork. Wonderful!

Christian poured a small measure of the 1970 Sevenhill Cabernet Sauvignon into my glass. I lifted it toward the light and examined it critically, before pronouncing that I felt its deep rich claret colour was exceptional.

I swished the wine around the glass, and examined closely any minute granules of sediment that adhered to the sides. I lifted the glass to my nose, and inhaled. Splendid! Finally, the ultimate test, I drank. Exquisite! Good wood, a fine bouquet, and a long finish. Will be even better after being allowed to breathe for half an hour.

I like wine — collecting wine, that is. Cabernet Sauvignons mostly, although I've recently branched out into the Shiraz and Malbec varietals as well. I buy Hermitages to drink immediately. All Australian wines, nothing imported.

I have a very elegant, quite expensive, solid-pine wine rack in which I store my collection. Unfortunately, I don't have a house under which I can dig a cellar to properly store my wine — at the exact temperature, with the correct amount of darkness, and facing in the direction of the Barossa Valley — but I'm working on it.

The pride and unutterable joy of my collection is a Seppelt 1971 Cabernet (TT147), vintaged entirely from Cabernet Sauvignon grapes grown at Seppelt's Dorrien vineyard in the Barossa Valley. This wine won the Jimmy Watson Trophy for the best 1971 Vintage Dry Red Wine at the 1972 Melbourne Wine Show.

(For anyone who doesn't know — tut-tut — the Jimmy Watson Trophy is to wine as the America's Cup is to yachting. It's the big one. Numero Uno. The goldest of gold. You can see why Jimmy Watson and I might tend to be good friends.)

I don't drink the wine in my collection — I just collect it. I store it in my rack, and I look at it. I arrange it. I rearrange it. I straighten bottles. I pull bottles out and fondle them and stare misty-eyed at their labels. I gloat over the boasts of gold medals and red ribbons.

I talk about my wine. I use long words and unusual phrases, and I adopt a toffy accent. Often I don't know exactly what I'm talking about, but I make sure that the people I'm talking to know less about wine than I do. This allows me to make very important-sounding announcements without fear of interruption or contradiction.

I take great pride in my collection. For many months I have gone to extraordinary lengths to protect my wine from the ravages of *Mr Sheen* and feather dusters. Dust is very important — it shows age, refinement, distinction, and peace. I have even gone to the length of inviting spiders home to spin their webs between the bottles (a move that has not increased my popularity with my *Mr Sheen*-wielding, pathologically-spider-loathing wife).

I do all these things to my wine, but I don't drink it. It is too good to drink. It would be an abomination to see it actually gurgling down someone's throat. It would be sacrilege. If I want to *drink* wine, I tap a cheap cask.

Perhaps I'll never drink my wine. As each year passes, the value of the wine increases, and its quality, presumably, improves. Therefore, if I never drink it, the wine will be perfect and infinitely valuable. It was only that one bottle,

CABINET
SHEILA'S
1986

that Sevenhill, that I ever drank from my collection. It was exquisite, but when I'd drunk it, it was gone.

It could be that we do to Jesus what I've done to my wine. Maybe we've left him sitting on the shelf, real nice to look at, pleasant to analyse and made pronouncements about — valuable, special, but ultimately just sitting on the shelf, accumulating dust and cobwebs.

It could be that we're still doing the right thing and going into a church building occasionally to grunt out a few off-key hallelujahs. Maybe we can even clinically dissect a phrase of a verse of a chapter of a book of the Bible; but if that's where it stops, then we're really still leaving Jesus up there on the shelf.

Perhaps we put Jesus off to that time when we *really* need him, saying he'll be much more valuable *then*.

Being a Christian means taking Christ into your life, physically and whole-heartedly. Christ's invitation to take and eat and drink at the Lord's Supper is extended to all of us. It is the physical consummation of the relationship between Christ and us. It is the deepest and most significant and most mysterious relationship it is possible to have. Take and eat, take and drink.

In this communion, there is given the power, strength, and invigoration that we so desperately need as we trail about this planet. It is not enough to keep Christ at a discreet distance, adoring him from afar. Our relationship needs to be much closer. That's what Christ wants, and that's why he offers us his body and blood in the bread and wine of the Lord's Supper.

The worth of the wine that Christ offers is immense.
> 'Then he took a cup, gave thanks to God, and gave it to them. "Drink it, all of you", he said; "this is my blood, which seals God's covenant, my blood poured out for many for the forgiveness of sins" ' (Matt. 26:27,28).

I've still got my Jimmy Watson sitting in the wine rack at home. Let's not do the same to Jesus.

The case of the threatened follicle

I don't remember any more how old I was when I first found it. It must have been 13 or 14 or 15 or 16. Whatever age it was, I know I remember that I thought it was the biggest, most important experience of my life to that time.

I was so proud, I nearly burst. I wanted to strut around, in an open-necked shirt, to show everyone what a real smart and mature young fellow I was to get one of these.

It was great! Fantastic! Wow! And a hundred other leftover sixties-type words. I washed it. I polished it, I perfumed it.

I was very cautious and very careful with it. I would let people look at it, but touching was a no-no. It was mine, all mine, and you keep your greasy mitts off it. Get your own if you're so keen on touching one.

I suppose you've guessed what I'm talking about — have you? If you haven't, what I'm talking about is . . . is . . . (This is a dramatic little pause to create some suspense — it is the scene in the 1948 black-and-white horror movie, where the camera lingers on the delicate innocent young maiden brushing her long thick hair in the mirror, while in the background ominous music grows steadily louder, and a shadow suddenly falls across the floor, and the delicate innocent young maiden turns, and the music reaches a horrifying crescendo, and the shadow draws itself up straight, and the delicate young maiden screams and — are you riveted to the chair in suspense yet? No? Well, we had better wait a few more lines then______________________

____

Stop! That's enough — if you're not frozen with suspense by now, you never will be. What I'm talking about is . . .) is . . . my very first, my number one, my absolutely-never-seen-before-in-my-whole-life-about-my-own-person type experience — my first chest hair.

Yes. There it was. From out of nowhere. Without warning. My first chest hair. Joy of joys! O thou tender budding thing. Thou delicate creature. From where didst thou spring, thou first-fruit of manhood? Who hast made thee to bend so sweetly before me? (It's amazing how you rave on when you get your first chest hair.)

I thought it was dirt, first, and it wasn't until I'd rubbed my skin bare with scrubbing brush and Solvol that I realized it wasn't. It was a beautiful hair. I felt very attached to it.

But alas! This happy story strikes trouble. The hair was threatened. Right down to its follicle, the very root of its existence. Naturally, I leapt to its defence.

When that dastardly fiendish evilly-grinning former friend attacked me with the disposable cigarette lighter that day on the beach, I fought. I fought bravely. I rolled away, I threw sand, I hid under beach towels, I tried to run. I called for a lifesaver, I called for mercy. I tried to reason, I tried to placate, I tried to bribe. I begged. Got down on my knees and sobbed. 'Not the hair. Please. Anything but the hair!'

It was no use. The monster wouldn't listen. Bigger and stronger than me, it — yes, I can only call it 'it' — attacked without remorse. Pinned my arms and sat on my chest. Smiled leeringly. Flicked a flame on the lighter. Looked down at my hair. I blew out the flame. I got thumped. The flame again. I blew it out again. I got thumped again. Harder this time. Then, quickly, a flame, a sizzle, a puff of smoke, the smell of burnt hair, and it was gone. Finished. Ashes.

I lay there, very still. Hairless, I felt naked. Empty. As if I'd lost the most important thing I'd ever had. As if I'd lost everything. As if I had nothing.

That's just about how we line up for the grave. Naked. With nothing. Just like we came into the world.

We may spend our whole life accumulating things — three or four shiny mag-wheeled cars, every heavy-metal record ever made, a good job, trendy clothes, the whole bit. Maybe we get real rich or real famous or a real lot of friends. None of it can make it over that last border. We go naked. Status symbols aren't transferable.

The Pharaohs in Egypt tried. They killed a million-or-so slaves getting pyramids built for themselves. They stocked these giant tombs with enough wives, concubines, servants, perfumes, clothes, chariots, and riches to make sure they had a good time when they reached the other side. All that happened was that some pyramid-robbers got rich. Even the pyramids themselves are being weathered away.

Getting as attached as I did to that first hair on my chest is about as stupid as getting hooked on worldly goods, status symbols, and all those other material things we try so hard to gain. When you get to the grave, they mean absolutely nothing. Ashes to ashes, dust to dust.

In *Hamlet, Prince of Denmark*, Bill Shakespeare has a scene where Hamlet meditates at Ophelia's graveside. Hamlet spends most of his life meditating and soliloquizing; but Ophelia was his girlfriend, so what he says here gets pretty interesting. Hamlet talks about what death does to a person, and concludes that even the body of an important man like Alexander the Great could end up being used to plug up the holes in the walls of a peasant's house. That's a pretty fair assessment, I reckon. So what use are all the things of this world then?

Jesus tells the parable of the rich fool who spent his whole life setting up things so that he could retire and have a rip-roaring time. What a black comedy! — the night he retires, he dies.

There was another rich man, a young one, who came to Jesus and asked what he should do to be saved. He thought he was all right because he reckoned he'd kept all the commandments. When Jesus told him to sell all his goods, give away all his money, and then to follow Jesus, the man ran away. Riches have a way of trapping you.

Listen to what Jesus says:
> 'Do not store up riches for yourselves here on earth, where moths and rust destroy, and robbers break in and steal. Instead, store up riches for yourselves in heaven, where moths and rust cannot destroy, and robbers cannot break in and steal. For your heart will always be where your riches are' (Matt. 6:19-21).

So, whether it's hairs on your chest, or the car in your driveway, or the balance in your cheque account, be careful. Don't get too attached to it — you can't take it with you. Store up your riches in heaven. They're safe there, and they'll be waiting. With God.

The young person's guide to an evening at the pub disco

There was a very nasty incident at the pub last night. It was something I've never experienced before. Quite unprecedented and quite drastic. It caused a mighty stir. It only lasted a moment, probably no more than a split second, but it happened. There was silence. People could hear what the person alongside them was saying. Communication occurred. It was a disaster of massive proportions.

I don't know how it happened. Perhaps the deejay fell asleep, or misjudged his tapes. Whatever it was, it was a bad mistake, and even now he's probably looking for a new job. When it happened, though, there was no time for thought, only a mad moment of panic as he tried to find the 150 decibels he needed to kill any chance of conversation. When he did find it, everyone was able to relax again. They went back to their practice of opening and closing their mouths in pretend-conversation.

Pretend-conversation is really very useful. You can substitute anything you like for the spaces that the other person's mouth indicates. You can be chatted up all the time. You can be the world's best teller of jokes. You can be intelligent. Or, if it looks as if you could be getting into trouble, you can say, or pretend to say, that you were saying: 'Excuse me'.

Actually, most people don't pretend-say, they pretend-shout. And when everyone is shouting, that's a lot of drinks — no, it's not, it's a bad joke, sorry! What I mean is that there is a lot of noise. This of course means that everyone has to shout even louder to be heard, which means that everyone else has to shout even louder, which means — I think you can see what it means. It's the reason that they have the music so loud — so that people can't hear their ears bleeding.

I don't know how they calculate the capacity of pub discos. Whatever method they use, it is blatantly wrong. It seems that they think the average person only needs four square centimetres of space, and they don't allocate a centimetre more. And in their allocation they forget to allow for the space that the tables and chairs use up, although this is not a major problem because they only allow ten seats per thousand people.

I always thought that the object of dicos was dancing. I was wrong. There is no such thing as a dance floor. There is only one's four square centimetres. The only dancing that is done is a sort of swaying from the ankles up. This is to avoid elbows, drinks, and lit cigarettes.

Some people enjoy breathing. These people should not go to pub discos. Oxygen is in short supply at pub discos. It is not unusual to see the hard-of-breathing wearing scuba gear in order that they might inhale something other than thick blue smoke and McDonalds breath.

In recent times, deejays have got themselves another toy to play with. It is a video screen that slides up and down the wall whenever they want to use it. The screens are huge, and they flash a bright colour. The deejay either puts on the film-clip of the song that's being played, or some other appropriate piece of film. (Before we go any further, would you please place inverted commas around 'appropriate'.)

Maybe I'm old-fashioned, but I really fail to see — with very wide-open eyes, mind you — what a parade of Miss World contestants in swimming suits has to do with a monotonous disco song. Especially when underneath the contestants are the scores the judges have awarded them.

For the boys in the pub it's just a perve session. They award the contestants a score too, but I think their judgment is based on the size of the swimming gear. Miss Honduras, with a swimsuit cut so high above the hips that it only reappears at the armpits, is a runaway winner.

Like the loud music, the video screen tends to kill conversation. Everyone turns to face it, and I don't know if you've ever noticed but it's pretty difficult to carry on a meaningful conversation with the dandruff-flecked back of someone's head. It's funny the way giant electric faces are more interesting than the real live ones next to you.

People worry about young people getting drunk in pub discos. Maybe young people *do* get drunk, but it beats me how they manage it.

First, every drink is so expensive that you have to work a week to be able to afford more than one. And don't think a soft drink is any cheaper — it costs less to have a beer.

Second, you have to reach the bar. When a pub is crowded, there is a mob ten deep at the bar. People have died of thirst before they've been able to reach it. You practically have to step over the bodies of drought-stricken weaklings who did not have the strength to make it.

Third, even if you manage to get to the bar and are able to afford the drink, you have to get the barperson to hear you. It can take hours, and even then you'll probably end up with something completely different from what you ordered. And it's always more expensive, and tastes awful.

Finally, after coping with all that, there is only a one-per-cent chance that you'll get your drink safely back to your spot without having most of it accidentally tipped all over you.

You'll find, too, that because there is so much pushing and shoving in pub discos that the 'glasses' are actually made out of plastic. I don't know about you, but, to my palate, a 'plastic' of beer just doesn't taste the same.

Have I mentioned bouncers yet (or 'Security', as they prefer to call themselves)? They're the ones with short haircuts and big muscles. They wear tight T-shirts with the hotel's name on it, and they have lots of scars and tattoos. They charge you a hundred dollars to get in, and then stamp your wrist with an ink that is impossible to remove. They do this so that they can grab your arm and abuse you when you try to step outside for a breath of fresh air, or to use a packed convenience.

After all that, you have your good time. You can't breathe, you can't hear, you can't drink, you risk bodily damage, and you pay lots of money for the privilege. I can handle that experience occasionally — especially if there is a good band playing — but I cannot understand how people do it every week, and three or four times a week.

You can go to a pub disco and have a good time. And you don't need to get drunk or picked up, either. Maybe, from the outside, it seems that pubs and discos are terrible dens of iniquity, but, if a person has any common sense and self-control at all, they don't have to be. And I expect a Christian to have a fair amount of both of those qualities.

I think it's important that we stay in touch with the people around us. You can lock yourself away in an ivory tower and be perfectly safe, but you're also perfectly useless. If you can connect with other people on a person-to-person basis, then maybe that will go some of the way to showing other people that Christians are real people too. Christians, too, might like a drink of beer or a rum and coke, or the sound of a full-on rock'n'roll band, or the company of the opposite sex. And the pub disco seems to be the only place where these three are present together.

Christians need to show people what they have in common with them, and then to show the extra dimension that faith in Christ gives them. They can help others to see that the abuse of sex and alcohol and people is a crazy way to try to meet your needs, when the way of Jesus is available. And that's why I think that there is a place in the pub for a Christian young person, as long as he or she is responsible enough not to abuse it. That's what *I* reckon, anyway.

Junk mail

Maybe it's just our letterbox.

Admittedly, it's not a particularly special-looking letterbox — just a few bits of buckled wood banged lopsidedly together and then slapped with a few splashes of Mission Brown Fenscote, but maybe, beneath that humble frame, there is something special. Perhaps our letterbox has a sinister past, has committed some crime, in the dark distance of yesterdays, for which it is still being punished.

There has to be some explanation for the phenomenon. If it's not the letterbox, what else could it be? Surely not me?

Whatever it is, action has to be taken. I am sick and tired of having to wade through a front yard littered with junk mail that has overflowed from the letterbox. There is no way I am going to continue chasing tearaway bits of paper waltzing down the street like school-kids just let out for holiday.

Junk mail.

We get: full-page grocery-special spreads from 70 supermarkets;

full-colour 50-page catalogues from variety stores, advertising dollar dazzlers and cent sizzlers;

fake hand-written cards from 240 local real-estate agents, each with a queue of 47 people knocking each other on the head to try to buy our house first (a house we only rent);

cheap home-made handbills (photocopied down at the local library) advertising discounts at the local hair-hackers;

special free vouchers for use at the international chain takeaway food place (you buy 15 dollars' worth of chicken and you get a chip free);

post-paid envelopes from a charity a day;

school-kids' icecream sticks and leftover sandwiches;

and a dozen or so local papers (each containing one item of news — usually about the primary school — and two million ads).

That's a lot of junk mail. And that's just normal times during the year — it's not even Christmas or New Year, or Pink Pigeons' Day, or any of those other times when they give things an extra push.

Junk mail must work, or otherwise the industry wouldn't keep growing. I suppose the advertisers feel that they can trap people in their own homes — they *have to* pull the junk from the letterbox, therefore they *have to* at least glance at it, therefore there *must be* the *chance* of a sale.

Now, while one problem with junk mail is its volume, and another is its bulk, the worst problem is that of trying to find the *real* mail among all the junk. I don't get a lot of letters, but when I do get one, I love it. I spend most of my day dashing out to the letterbox to see whether the postie's been.

It's hard to tell whether he has or not. You have to search and search through all the dross before you find the letter you've been hoping for, the only one of any value. And you have to be very careful that you don't accidentally throw *it* out with all the junk.

God's Word is a sort of letter to us. It's a letter that is real and valuable, and it contains a message that we need to hear. The trouble is that it is terribly easy for this letter to get lost among all the junk that comes our way.

The junk comes from a million directions. It comes from the people who say that the only thing that matters in life is the latest haircut. Or from the boss who tells you that anyone who isn't a boss is a nothing. Or from the media that says that, unless you're young, lithe, tanned, and look sexy in a tiny swimsuit, you've got no right to be in this world. Or from the alcohol and tobacco companies that say that unless you use their products (to excess, though they'll never say *that* out loud) you're unattractive, and out of it. Or from the

26

scientists who preach that they have conclusively proved that God does not exist, and that therefore it is time to have faith in them and all their fun little experiments that have managed to put humanity on the brink of holocaust. Or from the political parties that say: 'Vote for me. I'm honest. I'll save you.' Or from the banks that promise to fulfil all your dreams with their money — at a cost. Or from all the other places it would take too long to list.

This is junk mail that comes and comes, and doesn't stop coming. It's not really feasible to try to hide from it, or to hope that somehow you can find a way to tell it to stop. We live in this world, and we can't escape coming into contact with its junk. What we have to do is to throw it away when we get it. Get rid of it. Don't even take a little look at it.

The other thing we have to do is to make sure that we don't throw out God's message to us along with all the other stuff. We have to keep God's message close to us, inside us.

Stop looking at the junk this world throws up, and start looking into the Bible. Read the message of hope that God is sending, and accept it. When you sift through the junk of the world, you'll find the jewel of God.

The best way to finish this off is to look again at what I reckon is a pretty fair summary of God's message to us in the Bible. It comes from the Gospel of John, and is a message that we can all carry around with us, all the time, wherever we go.

> 'For God loved the world so much that he gave his only Son, so that everyone who believes in him may not die but have eternal life' (John 3:16).

The exposure of a flashing half-back flank

I had a very nasty accident today.

It happened as I was bending down to retrieve something I'd dropped on the floor — in the full view of a major gathering of friends and relations. A ghastly ripping sound. A brush of cold wind. I clutched my belly. This is the end, I thought. My hernia op. stitches have split. My insides are going to fall outside. This is the end of my short time on this earth.

Well, it wasn't quite the end, but it concerned my end. My jeans split. From top to flashing bottom. My half-back flank was completely exposed. I was completely mortified.

That's about the first time I've ever split my pants. I didn't split the jeans because I had suddenly become terribly overweight in the buttock (great-sounding word, that one) region, but because my jeans were approaching their bicentenary and were worn practically transparent.

That's something I've noticed lately — all my jeans have suddenly got old and begun sprouting patches on their knees like moles on a chin. And I don't care.

When I get up in the morning I'm such a wreck that I just throw on whatever is lying around. I'm not real great with colours, so apparently I rarely match. But I don't know, so I don't mind. I don't even mind wearing air-conditioned shoes held together with a rubber band that keeps on breaking. I like shoes that look like a thirsty dog, hanging out its tongue for water.

I never used to be so sloppy about my appearance. I used to take a great deal of care. I realized that I was never going to look like the cute lead singer of whatever pop band was in vogue at the time, and that I'd have to compensate in clothes for what my face lacked.

So I bought proper clothes — ones on which the maker sticks his or her initials in the most blatant position, so that everyone can see who they're made by and therefore how much they're worth. If I wore jeans, they were Levis —never the el cheapo Four Star brand. I polished my shoes. I wore matching jocks. I brushed teeth, shampooed hair, showered in aftershave, even cleaned my fingernails. I used to do everything I could to get myself looking as good as it was possible for someone as ungood-looking as me to get.

I can't remember if I liked doing all that, if I actually enjoyed dressing up, or whether I reckoned attracting the opposite sex was worth that cost. Whatever the reason, I did it.

I don't know what happened to all that idealism and care. I've got slack. Maybe it *was* all just to impress the opposite sex; now that I'm married, that's a no-no. And I'm not interested in it, anyway.

When you live with someone for a while, you begin to get comfortable with them. You relax, and you let fall some of the barriers you used to hide behind. You don't feel the need to put on a big act to cause an impression any more.

Of course, I *do* get dressed up sometimes, to go out to dinner and things. It makes a nice change; and if I'm lucky and my wife's not looking too closely, I might even score a compliment or two. Dressing up feels special, then; it's not an effort, it's a privilege.

Maybe the first thing you ever remember learning about God was that he was a God that you had to impress. You may have come scampering out of childhood thinking that God was very big and very powerful and got mad at the slightest misdemeanour, and that you had better watch your step unless you wanted to get into deep trouble. You had to go out of your way to impress God, to show him that at least you were worth saving. You had to show him that you were basically a pretty good sort of person, the sort of person who would fit easily into the scheme of things in heaven without requiring too much forgiveness and changing along the way.

If your first impression of God was like that, after a while it was probably modified and you started to compromise a little. You may have begun to ease up just slightly, to relax a bit, to slow down the tempo. Maybe you took a Sunday or two off from church each month, to go camping with your friends, or to watch the World of Sport replay, or just to sleep in after a heavy Saturday night. You got a bit slack with your prayers, just flinging a thought or two God's way when you had a bit of a problem on your hands. You knew that God loved you, and forgave you, and did everything to make you right with him — so you just leaned back and let him do it, while you got on with doing the things you wanted to do.

These are two extremes in our attitude toward God, and what we have to try to do is steer a way between them, to find a balance between thinking we have to do everything we can to impress God and win forgiveness, and doing nothing at all in response to God, out of laziness and contempt. That's not easy. It sounds like what I used to hear echoing about Sunday-school rooms as the balance between 'the Law and the Gospel'. Compare these two impressions of God that the Bible gives us:

> 'You shall worship no other god, for the Lord, whose name is Jealous, is a jealous [impassioned] God' (Exod. 34:14 RSV);

> 'God showed his love for us by sending his only Son into the world, that we might have life through him. This is what love is: it is not that we have loved God, but that he loved us and sent his Son to be the means by which our sins are forgiven' (1 John 4:9,10).

We are faced with both of these scriptural views of God. We recognize that God is a powerful God and one who deserves worship. On the other hand, we know that God is a loving God who has made it easy for us to come before him, by the forgiveness Jesus has won for us.

Therefore, our attitude to God will be one of respect and admiration, and also love and gratitude. We can be comfortable with God, but we must also retain our respect. We can call God 'Dad'. We can talk to him about anything. We can be easy and relaxed. But we can't take it so far that God becomes nothing more than a convenience, to be used for our purposes when, and only when, we want him. Our respect for God protects us from that.

It's good to be comfortable in a relationship. It's also good still to want to do things to impress and please your partner. Maybe I should get dressed up for my wife more often, buy some new clothes. I really should chuck these jeans out — they *are* dead. Maybe I could give my wife a surprise: shave before she comes home, get dressed up, take her out to dinner. Yeah, that would be good — I just feel like McDonald's.

Johnny's cubby

It would be the best cubby-house in the world, and everyone would have to agree, including Jimmy, and even cranky Mrs Jones next door. Johnny had drawn up all the plans and coloured them in, and they looked really nice, and Johnny's dad said they were excellent.

He offered to help Johnny build his cubby, but Johnny wanted to do it all by himself. His dad could come in and share it when it was finished. Johnny's dad said: 'All right. But if you need any help, remember, just ask.'

The first thing Johnny did was dig a foundation. At least, he would have dug a foundation if he could have got that great big spade into the very hard dirt underneath the gum tree in the back yard. When he couldn't manage it, he said: 'Blow it — I won't have any foundations. She'll be right.'

Next, Johnny got some of his dad's garden stakes to make the corner posts of his cubby. He had to steal one that was holding up a tomato bush because he could only find three in the shed. After a lot of work, he managed to get them to stand up, and he stood back and looked and thought what an excellent job he'd done.

The next job was to build walls, and Johnny had a brainwave — he'd use the corrugated iron from the old chook shed down in the back corner of the yard. Getting the iron off was easier said than done, and Johnny cut two fingers and hurt his backside before he managed it, but he didn't cry because he was trying to do everything by himself.

Johnny leaned the tin up against the stakes, and felt very pleased with himself. He stayed very pleased until the dog came charging round the corner, gone mad after the cat, and crashed into a corner stake. The whole lot went flying into the air. Johnny would have got mad and drop-kicked the dog a block or two, but it was already half a yelping kilometre down the street.

Johnny got his dad's hammer out, so that he could nail the iron to the stakes. He had seen his dad use the hammer, and it was so easy that even a child could do it. Johnny tried. He missed the nail, hit his thumb, and jumped a metre in the air. He tried again, and knocked down the stake. Johnny decided the hammer was broken, so he put it in the rubbish bin. He'd tie the iron to the stakes with string.

The construction so far wasn't the most solid building ever seen, but at least it was up. All it needed now was a roof. The only thing that Johnny could think of that would be big enough was the family tent. They only used it at Christmas, and it was a long time until then, so ...

Johnny had to cut some pieces off the tent, and it got a big tear in it where it caught on the iron, but it worked. And the cubby was finished. There was no time to play in it, though, because it was dark now and time to go inside.

There was a storm that night — strong wind and heavy rain.

The next morning, before his dad could even have his toast and vegemite for breakfast, Johnny dragged him down to the backyard to look at the cubby. When they reached the gum tree, they both stopped.

There was no cubby. There were pieces of tent flapping in the branches of the gum. There were sheets of corrugated iron in the vegie patch. There were broken stakes. But there was no cubby.

Johnny began to cry, and his dad nearly did, too, when he saw the tent, but he was too kind. He put his arm around Johnny's shoulder and told him not to worry. He said they would build a cubby together.

Johnny's dad showed Johnny how to dig deep foundations, and how to build strongly. They worked together. Johnny's dad did the hammering, and Johnny did the holding; but Johnny's dad pretended that Johnny was doing nearly all the hard work.

They finished the cubby just after lunch. It was strong. It was solid. It was fantastic. It was the best cubby Johnny had ever seen, and it was easily the best in the world. Johnny was very happy, and he went inside his cubby. He started arranging things, then rearranging them, and then putting them back where they were before. He was having a terrific time.

Later on that afternoon, Johnny's good friend Jimmy came over. He looked at the cubby long and hard, and said he thought it was probably the best cubby in the world, and could he come in.

Johnny said No. He said he had built the cubby all by himself, and his dad had helped just a little bit, and now it was all his and his dad's, and no one else was allowed in because they might mess it up. Jimmy went home, sad.

Jimmy came around the next day, after school, and asked if he could go in the cubby. Johnny said No again. Jimmy kept coming around, every day for a whole week, but Johnny kept on saying No. Finally, Jimmy didn't come around any more.

Johnny played in the cubby for another day or two, but it started to get a bit lonely in there. He had no one to talk to and to play games with, and he wished Jimmy would come around. But Jimmy didn't.

The next day, at school, Johnny asked Jimmy over. He said he had decided to let Jimmy come into his cubby because Jimmy was his best friend and Johnny knew that he wouldn't mess up the cubby.

Jimmy just laughed, and said he didn't want to come over. He had his own cubby, now. And his was bigger and better than Johnny's.

Johnny's cubby is empty and dark, now. Johnny doesn't play in it any more, because he doesn't know what to do in there all by himself. No one goes in it at all — except spiders and, occasionally, the dog. The cubby sits there alone, empty and silent. As if it is dead.

A long way from home

The day never really dawned. It had poked its head tentatively through the curtain of rain that hung down everywhere. The sun refused to shine. It had rained all night, and it looked as if it would rain all day. There had already been 60 mm in the previous 24 hours.

It did rain all day.

It was now dusk, and I was driving home. It had been a miserable day, and I was tired and cold. I just wanted to be home. The trip usually took 40 minutes, but tonight it had already taken an hour and I was only half way home. Water had played havoc with traffic lights and had in places flooded the road. Traffic had built up. I only had ten kilometres to go, on a three-lane highway, but the traffic jam showed no sign of moving.

Darkness began to fall, and the rain kept beating down. I turned up the radio, but the sound of the rain was louder. The deejay shouted out jokes about seeing an old man with a white beard herding animals toward a large boat moored at the marina.

Like my temper, the temperature gauge on the dash kept moving further and further into the red. The traffic hadn't moved for 20 minutes.

I tried to keep a window open a little to let in some fresh air, but too much water came in. The windows fogged up. The radio clogged the air that was left. The darkness and the rain merged, and formed an impenetrable barrier. I knew there were cars and people all around me, but I couldn't feel them any more. I felt separated from them. I was alone, distant, a long way from home.

Time wore on, and my feeling of separation intensified. I began to feel that I would never get home. The radio said that the rain had caused major flooding. It read out a list of the roads that were impassable, including the one I was on — a bridge had been washed out. All the alternative routes I knew were flooded as well.

I became quite frightened. I began to realize how important home was — how it was a base, a centre to work from and to work around. It was like having a still point in a crazily-spinning world. I felt strong bonds with it. Not just the people. Not just my pipe, or my favourite chair. Or my books and mementoes. It was the idea of home, the idea of having somewhere to go, of not being lost. My place. Home as a sort of definition of who I am, of what I am doing, where I am going. A symbol of love, comfort, security.

I eventually made it home. Three hours later. With a piece of the best dare-devil driving you're likely to see outside of Le Mans, and thanks to the kindness of a few drivers more patient than myself, I managed to squeeze my way out of the traffic jam. I back-tracked a few kilometres, and then picked a way through the less flooded of the back roads and suburban streets, until I could find a clear route home.

That feeling of separation from home must be something like the feeling refugees have as they enter a new country. I was separated by only a few kilometres and for only a few hours; they are separated by thousands of kilometres, perhaps for ever. And there is not only the distance involved, but also the difference in language, culture, and appearance, and the loss of friends. What longing for home, what loneliness, and what fear must there be? We should do anything we can do to help those seeking refuge in Australia to feel at home.

The Australian Aboriginals too, the original walkers of this land, with their affinity for it, must feel terribly alienated when separated from it.

This sort of physical separation is tragic enough, but even that does not compare with the tragedy of the separation that sin has caused between God and humanity. Compare the paradise Adam and Eve experienced in the Garden of Eden in harmony with God, to the harsh reality of separation they had to face after sinning.

In the same way, when we are cut off from God, who is our home base, our source of strength, then we drift aimlessly and helplessly in a world that can be terrifying if we feel we're all alone. Separation is dark and lonely, and it hurts.

God recognizes the tragedy of separation. To overcome it, to make it possible for us to be joined to him again, he gave his Son Jesus. Jesus paid the price of our sin. He brought us back, he brings us back. He is the bridge over all the troubled waters that flow between us and God. Jesus is the Shepherd that goes out into the night to find and bring home the one sheep out of the hundred that was lost.

There's an old bumper-sticker that you've probably seen plastered on a beat-up Volkswagen around the place somewhere, that says: IF GOD SEEMS FAR AWAY, GUESS WHO MOVED? Maybe the message has been repeated so often that it's a cliché now, but the statement it makes is still valid, and it does point us back to look at our relationship with God. God doesn't move away from us; it is we who move away from him. God is there waiting for us when we return. That's reassuring, but doesn't it make a lot more sense not to move away in the first place?

Psalm 23 is probably the best-known psalm in the Bible, and that's probably because its message is so vital and so relevant to so many people. It is a message of hope and faith and praise. It's the sort of message that can pierce the gloom we might sometimes feel when we're a long way from home.

> 'The Lord is my shepherd;
> I have everything I need.
> He lets me rest in fields of green grass
> and leads me to quiet pools of fresh water.
> He gives me new strength.
> He guides me in the right paths,
> as he has promised.
> Even if I go through the deepest darkness,
> I will not be afraid, Lord,
> for you are with me.
> Your shepherd's rod and staff protect me' (Ps. 23:1-4).

The surprise Christmas present

The box was big enough to hold anything from a washing machine to a lawnmower. It was brown, and tightly secured with masking tape and string. It sat on the lounge room floor and asked a thousand questions. What? How? Why? From where? From whom?

It was Dad's Christmas present to Mum, back in 1969.

Us kids had already received ours — we didn't have the patience that Mum did. While we were quite happy and contented with our new footie, or new Barbie Doll, or big block of chocolate, we couldn't sit still until the surprise and mystery of that big brown box had been explained.

So we badgered Mum until she began unwrapping.

Dad sat in a corner chair, pretending he wasn't at all interested. He had a smirk on his face, and weighed in regularly with the sort of wet jokes fathers are famous for. He had us expecting either a baby elephant or a new fishpond.

Mum got out the scissors and cut the string. Then she slowly peeled off the masking tape. She wasn't quick enough for us kids, so we all jumped up to help. The smirking father in the corner told us all to sit down. Mum continued her unwrapping, and pulled open the top of the box.

A three-metre barbed-wire fence would not have stopped the charge that followed. In the flurry of bodies that occurred, three of the four children in our family only just managed to escape serious injury from falling headfirst into the box. (Little sister was, at that time, *too* little to get much of a look-in.)

After the excitement had quietened down a bit, and we children had been pulled from the box, Mum showed us the smaller box she had discovered inside. Our curiosity grew. A couple of us had to go to the toilet. Everything stopped until everyone was present and accounted for. Dad interrupted to take a photo. We've still got it, and it shows all our noses six inches longer than normal. Even Nana and Papa leaned forward excitedly.

Inside the smaller box was another, and inside that still another. There was a noisy chorus of groans as still more wrapping was revealed. The process seemed as if it would go on for ever.

Eventually, Mum got to a very small parcel. It was wrapped in pretty pink paper, with a matching ribbon. This made it a stark contrast to the brown paper and newsprint which had preceded it.

Breath was bated. The munching of Christmas toffees stopped. The Christmas tree stood tall and elegant and silent. I even stopped punching my brother. All attention was focused on Mum, as she slowly unwrapped the pink parcel. Dad's smirk was changing to a smile.

Inside the parcel was a jewellery case. In it, a ring. A beautiful shiny ring. 'An eternity ring!' Mum whispered.

I thought she said *ma*ternity, and said that was a real surprise Christmas present.

Mum gave Dad a kiss, and I accidentally locked my brother in the big box and sat on it.

We took turns looking at the ring. It was a beautiful symbol of love, and a promise of future love.

There is a lot of wrapping around *our* surprise Christmas present.

The advent of God's Son is wrapped up in masses of tinsel along our crowded Christmas streets. It is submerged behind the fat red bellies and the fake white beards of the million-and-one jolly, ho-ho-hoing Santas doing the rounds in department store sleighs. It is disguised in Christmas cakes and puddings and turkeys and jars of chocolate-coated nuts. It is covered by layer after layer of office parties,

38

M E R R Y
C H R I S

after-work drinks, late-night shopping, and the card from one person we left off our list.

Even our 'Carols by Candlelight', our special Christmas Eve services, our warm feelings of special love and friendship and fellowship, are but more layers.

When all these layers are stripped away, then there is revealed the real gift, the real surprise Christmas present — the baby wrapped only in rags in a dirty stable in Bethlehem. This kicking, squirming baby is the Son of God born as man.

This gift is priceless. It is the measure of God's love for us. Its value far exceeds that of anything else we might ever receive, this Christmas or any other this side of eternity.

And as my Dad's gift of an eternity ring to my Mum was a symbol of love, and a promise, so is this child.

Yet this is more than just a symbol and an earthly promise. This is a real, unshakeable promise. This is love that can never be swayed by the vagaries of earthly life, a love that will not pass away in death. God's love, in this gift of his Son, *is* eternal — a true eternity ring.

Take hold of it and wear it. Know the love with which it is given and with which it continues to be given.

This Christmas, let's pay less attention to all the fancy wrappings, and more to the gift inside. Let's accept the gift of the Son of God into our lives. Then we can know the happiness of the best-ever surprise Christmas present.

Sunday

When I was a little kid, our family used to take holidays down the beach or up the mountains. We'd stay in a beat-up old caravan, and we'd have a good time. At night, a long way from a TV, we'd play cards or do jigsaws.

We had this one great jigsaw that was a map of Australia. It showed all the various industries in the different parts of the country. It had just the right degree of difficulty — not so hard that you could never get anywhere, but hard enough that it took a fair amount of time and a fair amount of brain to put it together.

The first time we did this jigsaw in the caravan, it was a real family affair — everyone helped. We moved along quite nicely and were soon within sight of the end, completion. As we got even closer, we began to suspect that something was wrong. Our suspicions were confirmed when we realized that the last piece was gone.

There was a major search — sleeping bags were tipped upside-down, rubbish bins were emptied, the floor was swept and the sweepings examined, pockets were inspected, cornflake packets were peered into, and every other conceivable place that the last piece of a jigsaw might hide in was searched. We found nothing. The piece was gone.

We looked at the jigsaw, and it looked pretty good. But no matter how good it looked, our attention was always drawn to the gap, the empty space, the flaw. It was only tiny in the context of the whole jigsaw, but it attracted all the attention. It was a flaw that destroyed the whole effect.

The same sort of thing can happen if you're dressing up for a big night out. You get all your clothes dry-cleaned, you stay in the bathroom for about four hours, you get everything immaculate — and then you notice it. The flaw. That one tiny flaw that destroys the whole effect — the dirty great pimple winking mockingly from next door to the left nostril.

The blood-curdling scream that usually follows this sort of discovery is potent enough to shatter the mirrors of every house in the street, and to send the pink-dressing-gowned lady across the road to 000 and hysterical tales of rape and mayhem.

When something is incomplete, or unfulfilled, it is an irritation, an eyesore, a problem, a frustration. It spoils perfection.

And that is how we as people are.

We don't have just one piece missing from the jigsaw puzzle that is our form. (Some of our forms are more a puzzle than some others.) We don't have just one metaphorical pimple on our nose. We are a mess of gaps and spaces and flaws that can't fit together in the harmony that a perfect person would be.

Human beings are biological, rational, spiritual, social and ... ahem, excuse me for raising this in our hedonistic world ... sinful. All these factors, these facets of being human, come together in one of an infinite variety of forms to make the person each one of us is.

How often don't we look at ourselves, recoil in horror, and say: 'If only ...' If only I were a bit less of this and a bit more of that. If only I had this talent — hair that could be gelled into that style, eyes that would look that colour in candlelight. If only I was better at mathematics, sport, singing. If only I could get rid of that habit, or that physical feature I inherited, or my raucous embarrassing laugh.

If I could, then I would be perfect. Or so close to it that I could give the movie stars a run for their money.

If I had it all together, the way I wanted it, I could show the world the *real* me. Not the me that gets distorted in all the imperfections that trap me, but the me I know I could be if I could get out from under my limitations. I could be fully human, and, because of that, fully alive. I could be anything and everything I want. Life would be mine. Life in all its fullness.

That may be our dream. Maybe we are able to recognize that we will never be this perfect specimen of humanity, the candidate for a Coca Cola commercial, but that doesn't stop us dreaming.

But there is another person that each of us *can* start to be. A person who *is* a full and total human being. A person who spends the hours allotted on this earth being *fully* alive.

This person is the person that God can make of us. This person isn't the product of a hundred-and-one courses in yoga or transcendental meditation, or a hundred-and-one cups of ginseng a day, or lots of carrots, or lots of tablets. This person is the one who believes and accepts Christ's offer when he says:
> 'I have come in order that you might have life — life in all its fullness (John 10:10).

In the 'days' of the 'week' that follow this one, I want to look a little closer at the various parts of me that make me the human being I am: the biological me, the rational me, the spiritual me, the social me, and the sinful me. I'd like to show the comparison between the person I will be if I live my life caught up in merely human conventions and ideals, and the person that I can be if I take Jesus up on his promise to give 'life in all its fullness'.

So, I'll see you 'tomorrow'.

Monday

Eating, sleeping, and breathing are a few of my favourite pastimes. Especially on Mondays. In fact, Monday a.m. I do little more than eat, sleep, and breathe.

I must enjoy eating, sleeping, and breathing, because I've been doing them for as long as I can remember. I'm sure I would be very sad if I had to stop doing any of them for any length of time. If I had to stop breathing, well, then, I don't think my life would be worth living any more.

As for eating, let me just say that God didn't give me a belly *this* size for it to remain empty. No, it was made to be filled. That large vacuous space above my belt and behind my navel seems to have no other role in life but to consume. If, by some mischance, I happen to ignore it for more than an hour or two, it begins grumbling. Not quietly and politely, but out loud, in the middle of company, whining and whingeing and squeaking and thumping. And that sort of thing is very embarrassing when you're trying to be romantic or intellectual or mature.

Sleeping is one thing I am good at. It is the sort of job I like — one where you can lie down on the job without having to feel guilty. I have become so good at sleeping that not even a jackhammer at 30 centimetres can rouse me. Not even the brightest sunbeam that the sun can throw through the venetians can wake me. Not even the coldest hand a wife can place in the middle of my warm cosy back can make me stop sleeping (I lie; yes, it can! If it wasn't for that cold hand, I'd spend most of my life in sheer blissful sleeping).

My talent at these various biological functions makes me an expert biological human being. Which means that I am fully alive when I have fallen asleep immediately after a huge meal and am breathing with earth-shattering snores.

If that is to be fully human, then so are animals, so are stones, and so are ABC newsreaders.

There is no doubt that my biology is *part* of my humanness, but it is definitely not the extent of my being human. Therefore, just being fully biologically alive does not mean that I am fully alive.

I need to admit my biological humanity, and I need to sustain it, but I don't have to be ruled by it. I do not have to be the servant of my appetite, I do not need to bow down to my need to rest, I do not have to worship even the urge to life itself. These are but part of my total self, and they should therefore be allocated a certain priority. They themselves should not be the arbiters of all my other priorities.

It is pretty easy to get caught up in worry over where the next Big Mac is coming from, or how on earth you are going to meet the repayments on the new compact-disc player. You might fret about how high your blood pressure gets when taken by the nurse in the tight white uniform. You can get involved in doing this and organizing that and preparing for something else just in case, and get yourself so busy looking after yourself that you forget that you are more than just a biological being, and that God is the one taking ultimate care of your biological needs, anyway.

Jesus shares a few words of advice about this, that can be a reassurance to us.

> 'For only a penny you can buy two sparrows, yet not one sparrow falls to the ground without your Father's consent. As for you, even the hairs of your head have all been counted. So do not be afraid; you are worth much more than many sparrows!' (Matt. 10:29-31).

> 'This is why I tell you not to be worried about the food and drink you need in order to stay alive, or about clothes for your body. After all, isn't life worth more than food? And isn't the body worth more than clothes? Look at the birds flying around: they do not sow seeds, gather a harvest and put it in barns; yet your Father in heaven takes care of them! Aren't you worth much more than birds? Can any of you live a bit longer by worrying about it?' (Matt. 6:25-27).

In other words, get your priorities right.

God gives us the opportunity to be fully alive because we can trust in him to provide us with all our biological needs — our food, shelter, and clothing. God knows every breath we take — he gives us every breath we take. What gain is there for us in worrying about these things?

We are able to explore the other avenues of our existence, to live fully the whole life God has given us, without becoming weighed down by concerns about mere sustenance. That is a wonderful freedom to have, and it is one to be valued in a society that preaches the exact opposite.

God is worthy of thanks for making the biological me free to be fully human and fully alive.

Tuesday

Human beings come off the production line equipped with a built-in brain as standard equipment.

It's a pretty marvellous piece of equipment, the brain. It is the central part of our nervous system, which allows us to come into intimate contact with our environment. It receives stimuli from our five senses, and by discriminating between these decides on appropriate action. The brain then sends a message of what it has decided to various other parts of the body via motor nerves.

The brain is enclosed by three membranes called the Pia Mater, the Arachnoid, and the Dura Mater. The biggest parts of the brain are two masses called the cerebral hemispheres. They communicate with each other and are the most highly developed parts of the brain, being responsible for the conscious and deliberate behaviour of the individual.

When we talk about the brain, we often refer to it colloquially as 'grey matter'. The grey matter is a mass of nerve cells.

It's a fascinating study to read about the brain and what it is capable of doing. I read somewhere once that we use only 5 to 10 per cent of the capacity of our brain. If that is so, it makes its possibilities seem limitless.

Already the brain has been used to create technology that enables us to joy-ride round the stars and take a stroll upon the face of the moon. It has allowed us to find means to store libraries of information in computers that keep getting smaller and smaller. It has given us the ability to repair many of the malfunctions of the bodies in which we live and breathe.

The achievements which the brain has allowed are very impressive. It would be very easy to have faith in the power and achievements of our rationality. It is tempting to make rationality into some sort of god — a god that will one day be able to solve all the problems of this life and even the ultimate problem: death.

That sort of starry-eyed vision is an exercise in naivety. We can do many wonderful things, but how often is it that we are able to control their consequences? We practise nuclear medicine to save lives, and we build nuclear weapons to wipe out entire nations. We spend millions to assist the creation of life through a test-tube, and we abort babies on demand. We spend billions on guns, while throughout the world people starve.

Our rationality does not extend beyond itself. It is caught in a small frame, it is shackled by selfishness, it sees no further than its immediate surrounds. It is blinkered and shuttered by personal prejudices. It is no basis for a god.

This hasn't stopped philosophers from using rationality as the base for a set of morals that excludes God. They have produced reams of essays that purport to show that we don't need God because we are capable of providing all the answers ourselves. They couch this idea in sentences like the following, from Immanuel Kant's *Groundwork of the Metaphysic of Morals*: 'Therefore nothing but the idea of the law in itself, which admittedly is only present in a rational being — so far as it, and not an expected result, is the ground determining the will — can constitute that pre-eminent good which we call moral, a good which is already present in the person acting on this idea and has not to be awaited merely from result'.

Do you want a few minutes breather after that?

I have so much trouble deciphering the big words and the complicated grammar that I don't even dream of arguing with the points made by philosophers such as this one. I believe God gave us a basically simple message, and that when we come across alternative statements as complicated as the one I have just shown you, then we have the right to question their worth, just on the grounds of their inability to be easily understood.

The simple fact is that we do *not* have the power in ourselves — in our rationality or in any other facet of our being — to be God. We cannot replace God with anything else. Our rationality can't even help us to get to know God — we accept God in faith. And faith is a child-like trusting thing, not the result of a decision made on the balancing of the pros and cons for the existence of God.

> 'Jesus said, "Let the children come to me and do not stop them, because the Kingdom of heaven belongs to such as these" ' (Matt. 19:14).

We have the words from Jesus' mouth — let our faith be like that of a child's.

We have been given a gift called rationality. It is a gift we can exercise with wonderful results. It has the potential to be used for enormous good, yet it can also be abused to cause enormous evil. We can use our rationality to serve, or we can fall into the trap of serving it.

Rationality is no god; it is a gift from God. It is just a part of the total me. It cannot explain, or replace, the faith God has given me. It is part of the fully human me, and, if used as God intended, will enable me to be, in coordination with all my other parts, fully alive.

Wednesday

What is a heart?

Is it just a muscle that pumps blood? Or the red blob stuck through with arrows on Valentine's Day cards?

What is a soul?

Is a spiritual life nothing more than a dark-corner affair with a bottle of Johnny Walker?

Am I just a pile of blood and guts held together by a mismatched collection of skin and bones?

Soul and spirit and heart all seem to merge into the one entity, but it is almost impossible to define just what we mean by them. Our limited language attempts to grasp the concept with approximations, like a butterfly net trying to capture air. Our words grab it and try to hold it, but ultimately fall away empty.

When I think of the spirit of a person I recall the reminiscence of one of my uncles. Maybe I've romanticized and distorted the incident through time, but as I recall it he came to the aid of my grandfather who had collapsed to a cold kitchen floor with a heart attack. My uncle said that he could *feel* the spirit of my grandfather leave his body, and after that he *knew* that my grandfather was dead.

Dr Elizabeth Kübler-Ross has done a lot of work on the experiences of people who have been in a near-death situation, and what she has reported tallies with what my uncle said.

Our spirit is a fire that was ignited at our conception. It is the life-spark that carries our essence. It is who we are. The dictionary describes it as the animating or vital principle of man, the intelligent or immaterial part of man, the soul.

My spirit is the me that bursts at the seams of this human body, that longs to escape the parameters set by my human frame and human condition. It is the life in me.

How defeating it must be, then, for those who believe that at death this spirit dies, that this flame is extinguished. That when our three-score-years-and-ten have passed, there is nothing but the cold damp stillness of the grave. Surely this is the sting of death, the victory of the grave.

For a Christian, the power of the grave is overcome, removed, obliterated. Christ has conquered death by his resurrection. This makes my resurrection certain — the flame that is me continues in eternal life with my Maker.

How can this conviction do other than show strongly and clearly in my earthly life?

How can I live a life that does not bear witness to this certain hope?

My confidence must simply ooze from me. I am not confined to this earth, to this dust in which I tread for a measured number of seconds. Through Christ I am eternal.

The time will come when I will depart this vale of tears, but that is a cause for rejoicing rather than sadness.

With this knowledge, my human life will also be a spiritual life. I will revel in my freedom to be, safe from the sting of death. I have confidence in Christ's resurrection, and so I have confidence in my resurrection.

I will nurture my spirit, feed it, draw into it the strength and hope of faith — faith given to me by the Holy Spirit, and nourished by God's Word and by the body and blood of Christ shared with me at his supper.

My spiritual life must enter into my day-to-day life.

It will change my nine-to-five routines into something new — the beginning of my eternal life. I will be a changed person. My life will be filled with a new dynamism, a new fire.

I will be more alive. This life I have been given will be transformed from a mere counting away of minutes into an energetic, ecstatic living.

There are others who subscribe to these same feelings of hope and dynamism, among them the existentialists. Their hope springs not from the certainty of resurrection but from the belief that people at their core are a nothingness, a void. Existentialists say they admit this and then use their life to fill this nothingness. They boast of a clear-sightedness and a hard-headed realism, but all they are really boasting of is their own narrow-mindedness and their desire to take a stance that will get them admired.

The Christian's dynamism is far greater and absolutely real. The Christian is filled with the certain hope of eternal life — no doubts. We don't need to pack our lives with events of note because we are afraid that there is nothing to follow. We live our lives to the full because our certainty of eternal life gives us the freedom to make of this life all that we can with what God has given.

Spiritual life, the certainty of continued life, makes me whole. It makes me fully human and fully alive. It enables me, when my earthly life is finished, to say, like my Saviour on the cross of my sin:
        'Father! In your hands I place my spirit!' (Luke 23:46).

This is my faith.

Thursday

Actually, as the last gasp of stinking smoke winds its way from the filthy ashtray into your eyes, stinging them, and as the heavy-metal band strikes its last pretentious clap-of-thunder chord, and as the last few bodies stagger from the sweaty dance floor, and as the alcohol works its pain on your skull, you begin to wonder why.

You wonder why you get dressed in your best busted Levis, pressed into the best tested pub design. Why you surrender your hard-earned money with little more than a murmur of thanks. Why you throw the alcohol down your rasping throat with no regard for its effect. Why all the talk is so loud and all the walk is so proud. And why, when it's all over, you still feel so utterly empty.

You try to convince yourself it was all worthwhile when the cold night air has slapped some colour back into your face, but the question remains: Why?

The answer is simply that we human beings are social creatures. We need each other. We are made to live and love with one another. We cannot be happy if we are always alone. We are not made to be hermits hiding in a cave, or in a two-room flat in a low-rent suburb, or even in front of a colour telly somewhere out in anonymous middle-class land.

The proof that we *are* social creatures is that there is so much loneliness in the world. Listen to your radio, read a book of poems, see a film. Over and over again there is a theme of loneliness, alienation, separation.

I can paint pictures of loneliness, too. If I wanted to, I could conjure up a ragged wino snoring on a broken bench in a windswept park. I could call to mind Meryl Streep, in black, at the end of a stone wall jutting into an angry sea. I could flicker a cheap black-and-white TV documentary of street kids selling their bodies for enough bucks to buy the next cap of heroin, so they can make it through the day.

That's just the 'romantic' loneliness, the loneliness that makes good art. What about the loneliness of a shy person in a crowded room? That of a wife alone with 'Days of Our Lives' while a smirking husband sips wine and clinches high-powered business deals and the hand of his secretary under the table?

But even they're still the clichés of loneliness, the ones we always point to. So then what? What about *my* loneliness? Those times when no one was willing to listen to me, to punch me on the arm and call me a 'silly bastard'? Those times when everyone laughed at the joke about me, and my cheeks burnt up in a pain I couldn't show? Those times when a song comes on the radio that makes me think of the times I felt so happy, so surrounded by friends — who have now all gone drifting off into the corridors of time? Does *that* loneliness count? Is that real?

We all know loneliness.

Sometimes it is only feeling sorry for ourselves. Sometimes it is our own stubbornness and determination to get our own way. Sometimes it is being let down by friends. Sometimes it is 'just me'.

Because we are social creatures, and because we all sometimes do get lonely, we go all-out to find enough friends to make us secure. Or we get married, and think that means the problem is solved. We like to pack away a few people to be friends for that rainy day when there's no one else around. We want to be safe from times of isolation. We put our trust in relationships, in people. We feel hurt when we are let down, betrayed, misunderstood. We feel bitterness and loneliness. No human friend can ever totally solve our loneliness.

Maybe you've guessed that this is where I come in with the line about God's friendship. Maybe you'll start sarcastically humming that little Sunday-school ditty, *'What a Friend We Have in Jesus'.*

All right. Maybe it does sound facile. And corny. It sounds too easy a solution. Too trite. Pat. Sort of spineless, sort of cissy. Very predictable for a devotion book. Not the sort of thing a thinking person should take much notice of. All right for down-and-outs, but not for well-adjusted, mature people.

If that's what you think, you're wrong.

God's friendship is strong. It is vital and alive. It is always present, but it isn't smothering. It doesn't stand you on your head and turn you into a 'Hallelujah, brother' mouther.

God's friendship gives you a secure base from which to explore relationships with other people. No longer do we need to look at others and measure what they can give to us; now we can offer to others the secure and certain person that God's friendship makes of us. We don't need to search for someone to fill all the gaps in our lives, because God has filled those gaps. We have already begun to live the happy and fulfilled life that such a relationship can create.

No longer the endless trek through hotels and discos and parking lots in search of the one-night stand that will translate into something more. We have our answer already. The words of Jesus: 'I will be with you always, to the end of the age' (Matt. 28:20) are our assurance. With that assurance we can be fully-alive social beings. And that's the sort of thing you'd like to share with friends.

Friday

Once upon a time there used to be a bad, naughty, evil thing called 'sin'. It affected everybody, and nobody liked it, and life wasn't very nice.

Sin didn't do anything for the long sun-tanned bodies in the Coca Cola commercials. It didn't improve the sound of the chromed exhaust on the hotted-up HQ with the overhead mags and twin-camshaft fox-tails. It couldn't be used to house overnight visitors in a three-bedroom brick veneer. It couldn't even be used like a credit card in the big department stores.

So sin was put out of fashion. It is now about as 'in' as sixties hippies, thermal underwear, and Malcolm Fraser (who?). And if something's out of fashion, it just doesn't exist any more, does it? Here, prove it for yourself; answer this question: When was the last time you broke one of the ten commandments? You don't know what the ten commandments are? The point is proven.

Sin went out of fashion when we discovered the 'good times', the 'new morality', 'liberation', 'rights for all', that 'guilt is a con job', and so on. We now know that sin — and its corollary, guilt — is 'just a bad feeling created and stimulated by the church seeking to maintain the authority and wealth of its oppressive regime'. Sin, so they say, is a 'fallacy', an 'outmoded concept', a 'bourgeois plot', etc., etc., etc.

Sin is something produced by wowsers to spoil our good times. It is the reason we have hangovers after a night of boozing. Sin, and the people who talk about it and point it out, are boring. Very boring. Boring, boring, boring.

Even for a Christian, sin is a bit of a problem. It is a very embarrassing thing to have to admit to — something like bad breath or an underarm perspiration problem. It's something you try to hide — from yourself and your friends. None of us likes to admit that we may be wrong, and being wrong is just about what sin is, basically.

So, we may try to ignore it. Forget about it. Go along with what the world tells us. Believe that sin is out of fashion, that it is an anachronism, that it doesn't exist any more.

Or we may go the other way. Go all neat clothes and short back-and-sides. Buy ourselves a soapbox, jump on top of it, far away from the 'filth' of the world, and preach to others the bad news about their sin and the good news about our perfection.

Neither way recognizes the truth about ourselves.

We are born sinful. There is no way we can get out of it, or around it, or past it. Sin is our legacy from Adam. And it doesn't stop there. We continue to sin every day of our lives. Without fail.

Sin separates us from God.

What do we do? Retire to a monastery and scrub floors and mumble Latin and forget to eat until we think we've earned enough forgiveness to get rid of the sin we've committed? Or maybe we should make a few 'generous' donations to the work of the church? Bury our heads in the sand of self-pity and 'Why me?' moaning? Or live it up and hope the whole thing's a hoax, as everyone keeps telling us?

Enter Jesus, stage right.

Jesus came into this world, and took its sin on his back. He carried sin to the cross, where he suffered and died so that we could be free of the punishment sin makes us deserve. Jesus won for us the forgiveness of his Father. Washed away the stain of our sin.

That's a neat simple little paragraph of words, but it describes the greatest deed of love this world will ever see. Think about that. Our sins are forgiven. We need only to admit our sin and seek forgiveness. It is freely available.

If you want to get all the lowdown on sin and God's grace, the best thing to do is to have a read of Paul's letter to the Romans. He explains everything clearly and succinctly.

People have a lot of trouble with accepting God's forgiveness. Some think you have to 'earn' it, like you have to earn all the other rewards in this life. They think you have to do a whole lot of good things first. I remember hearing or reading somewhere that someone put that view to Martin Luther. What he replied was in the form of a little story. He talked of an apple tree that was all gnarled and rotten. If, for some reason, it had good apples on it, could they make the tree healthy again? No, the tree must be strong and healthy first, and then it will produce good fruit.

There are other people who accept God's grace and think that, because they are forgiven, they can go out and sin as much as they like. There are others who think that, because they are forgiven, they can rest on their laurels and spend the rest of their life criticizing the sin of others. Wrong again! Read what Paul says:

> 'Sin must no longer rule in your mortal bodies, so that you obey the desires or your natural self. Nor must you surrender any part of yourselves to sin, to be used for wicked purposes. Instead, give yourselves to God, as those who have been brought from death to life, and surrender your whole being to him to be used for righteous purposes. Sin must not be your master; for you do not live under law but under God's grace' (Rom. 6:12-14).

We respond to God's forgiveness. We are grateful and we show it. We try to change our ways and clean up our act. We continue to call for forgiveness as we fail, and we witness, by our joy, to the freedom this forgiveness gives us.

We are still sinners in a sinful world, but no longer do we have to fear the results of sin. We don't need to find excuses or to try to explain it away with sociological or psychological jargon. We don't need to try to put it out of fashion. Christ has taken care of things. We are free to live in communion with God in the middle of this world.

While being fully human and fully mortal in our sin, we are at the same time fully alive in the forgiveness God gives us.

St John writes:
> 'But if we confess our sins to God, he will keep his promise and do what is right: he will forgive us our sins and purify us from all our wrongdoing' (1 John 1:9).

So there's a happy ending to the fairytale phrase beginning this collection of words — we *can* all live happily ever after.

Saturday

Saturday is the day on which the team that has trained hard and practised hard all week puts its theories to the test. A whole lot of fine and fancy ideas may have been worked out on a blackboard or by a computer; but until they're actually tried out in the hurly-burly of competition, you don't really know how successful they are. They may, for instance, be like the theories of my favourite football team: They look terrific on paper, and work well on the training track; but when it comes to the actual match, they usually get a decided 'wobble' before finally collapsing in a heap.

For the past 'week' I've rambled on about us being fully human, and I've looked in detail at particular aspects of our lives. Then I've shown how God can make our humanness fully alive. That's a great theory, and maybe you accept that it is God, who gives you faith through his Holy Spirit, that makes you a complete person — a person with a framework, a backbone, and the consequent strength and confidence that enables you to be a fully-alive Christian person in this world. But just how does all this go in practice?

Do you just stroll out into the street and say to the first punk rocker you trip across: 'G'day, mate! I'm fully human and fully alive', and then flash your neat new Christian smile? More than likely you'll be thought fully something completely different.

And what about when you don't feel like a fully-alive Christian? When you're low on bouncing-ball enthusiasm and excitement? What about the first time you're called a drag because you're a Christian? Or when you get retrenched? Or when your special friend gives you the flick? Or when you just can't scrape together enough energy to face the harsh sun of another day? Or when you roll into a church pew, and find nothing there but hollow people and hollow words?

So, what's happened to this person that is so fully human and so fully alive, so theoretically complete? What has happened to all the fire this person used to feel? Does God just get the credit for the good things, and unload the blame back on to us when things aren't perfect? Why can't things be perfect all the time?

The simple answer is that we're still human.

God's offer of fullness of life is always available. It doesn't expire after a certain period, or knock off at five, or take long weekends. God's there to pick us up whenever we come a gutser, to carry our load whenever it gets too heavy. We just have to call.

Even though we can accept that, it's still hard to know why we still have to go through doubts and difficulties and darkness. And again, the answer is that we're still human. We haven't been whisked away to some place in the clouds where we no longer have to come into contact with the world and with anything in it that might contaminate our 'fullness'. I am here, in the world, in the middle of others, living as a human being.

All right, it might be wonderful never to have any problems or failures, never to feel any doubt. It might be that we feel God has reneged on his promise because we *don't* experience a perfect life.

What we have to remember is that we're still people on earth, and the perfection we're looking for will only come about in heaven.

God has given us some time here on earth, and he promises us 'fullness of life'. He strengthens, guides and protects us, and makes it possible for us to experience a life that is fully alive, a life that no one but the person who accepts God can have.

It might be that we forget this sometimes, but God doesn't. So we have to ask him to help us. We have to demand God's love and strength — strength not to be ashamed, strength to work through doubts and fears, strength to recover from hurt. God gives it.

We can be the fully-human person each one of us is, and we can be fully alive, because Christ has come 'in order that you might have life — life in all its fullness' (John 10:10).

A mauler meets his match

I have just played in my first football match for five years. I have aches in places that I didn't know existed outside medical journals. I have become terribly aware that smoking is indeed a health hazard.

The football match in question was the biennial (it takes two years to recover from the previous one) grudge match between the Mill Maulers and the Despatch Destroyers. I played for the Maulers, the current holders of the coveted trophy — a flat, beat-up, autographed, old footy.

The word was out that the Destroyers were desperate for a win. In fact, the smart word had it that they had actually trained a number of times. Apparently, there had been team meetings, and each player actually knew where he'd line up on the field. We Maulers scoffed at this, because we were confident that our lack of preparation meant that we didn't need any.

When the day of the match arrived, it drew together the greatest collection of beer pots, dicky knees, and chain smokers seen since the last match. Someone had thoughtfully provided team jumpers that were long enough to cover most wounds, but unfortunately they had forgotten to tell a very important Under-7 team playing on an adjacent oval that we would require the changing rooms too. We got changed outside.

Our team was an interesting mixture of colour. While our jumpers were matching, there was an astounding variety of shorts, too gross to mention here. Only half the team had football boots — the rest wore thongs, desert boots, sandshoes, and even steel-capped workboots (which looked pretty funny hanging heavy at the end of matchstick legs).

The Destroyers had supporters, and a cacophony of car horns warned us that they had taken the ground. They

BF

jogged in a tight little group around the oval. This meant that we Maulers were obliged to do a warm-up lap, too. We straggled out on to the grounds in ones and twos, and, after shuffling a very few short strides, collapsed, as one, to the ground. This was to prove the highlight of our teamwork for the day.

We weren't allocated positions; we just wandered off to a vacant corner, or on to an opponent who looked smaller than us. Which is why the pudgy kid with red hair and glasses, the shortest person on the field, who thought he was out on a nature excursion and who had never played football in his life, ended up at centre-half-back. The centre-half-forward he was to play against was eight-foot-three, weighed twenty-five stone, and drove a semi-trailer. This position was to be one of the positions in which we Maulers fell down.

In the first quarter we gave the Destroyers a fright — we scored. Most of our team thought we'd won the game and were ready to hop into the stubbies. They were most disappointed when informed of the real situation.

The Destroyers soon recovered from their temporary shock and kicked ten or fifteen goals. It was in the course of one of these that our centre-half-back disappeared. Rumour had it that parts of him could be found caught in the stops of the centre-half-forward's footy boots, but no one was stupid enough to attempt to confirm this.

At quarter time we Maulers fell where we'd stood. It was only with some vigorous urging and the use of a number of stretchers that we were brought into a group. We would have discussed tactics then, except that we felt it was more important to breathe. The Destroyers stood around and shouted: 'Hubba, Hubba'.

The second quarter saw them increase their lead, and by half-time most of the Maulers were reaching for cigarettes and oxygen. The chorus of coughing that resulted could almost have been mistaken for a rousing display of enthusiasm. I can assure you that it wasn't. The Destroyers looked very fit, and someone said that they were last year's League Premiers in disguise.

I won't mention the third quarter.

Surprisingly enough, at three-quarter time there was some optimism in the Mauler camp — one of the Destroyers was seen sitting down. 'We've got them on the run', muttered one of our more inspired number.

Most of our team collapsed with cramp in the last quarter; I collapsed with rigor mortis. The final whistle was pure joy. As we staggered off the ground, our wingman commented that the next biennial event should be a game of darts. And as I examined my injuries, a mauled Mauler, I agreed.

It sometimes seems to me that the confrontation between Christians and the forces that oppose Christianity is about as one-sided as the Maulers versus the Destroyers. It seems that there are attacks being made on the validity of Christian values from every side.

Scientists seek to prove that God does not exist; and if they can't prove that, they try to replace him with their technology. Civil libertarians and groups campaigning for their 'rights' blame God and the church for what they call their 'oppression, suppression, and exploitation'. Academics crane their heads out from behind their books and dismiss Christianity as an anachronism, a decaying old-world structure, an outmoded artificial authority. Young people say Christianity is irrelevant and boring. The media loves to discover or create scandals. The whole image of Christianity is made up to resemble a senile teetering old grandmother babbling away in a distant make-believe world.

Against this is presented the image of a young, strong, vigorous, optimistic team of people working together to produce for themselves a perfect future, a brave new world free of the church and its morality, free of responsibility and free of God.

And if you're a Christian, that feels pretty daunting — something like staring into the mouth of a lion in front of a crowd of screaming Romans in a packed Colosseum. And I must admit that at times I get very angry with what religion has made of the church that God created. I get frustrated at endless trivia and petty disagreements and general gutlessness. At times I feel like throwing in the hymn book.

But I'm going to stick with it, because I know that Christianity is the only way forward for people, and I know that the church that has Christ as its head is the body of Christ on earth. Not only do I want to stand up to the forces that oppose Christianity from the outside, but I want to work at the weaknesses I see in the church from the inside. These are two areas where I have to work, where I have to fight, whatever the odds.

There are people who reject the church and Christianity because they cannot bear the opposition to it, or because they have become totally frustrated with the fallibility of the people who make up the Christian church. If you feel like that, I can only encourage you to take up the challenge, to try to remedy the problems you see. Because the church is made up of imperfect people, there will always be tensions and problems and strife. It is at these times that we must unite under Christ's leadership, and remember again the way Paul describes us as the church.

> 'Christ is like a single body, which has many parts; it is still one body, even though it is made up of different parts. In the same way, all of us, whether Jews or Gentiles, whether slaves or free, have been baptized into the one body by the same Spirit, and we have all been given the one Spirit to drink . . .
> 'And so there is no division in the body, but all its different parts have the same concern for one another. If one part of the body suffers, all the other parts suffer with it; if one part is praised, all the other parts share its happiness. All of you are Christ's body, and each one is a part of it' (1 Cor. 12:12,13,25–27).

That is what Christianity, expressed as the church, is: the body of Christ. Not buildings and organizations and people you don't like. If we can keep that as our guide, then together, with Christ as our head, we can face the threats of this world with the confidence that assures us that nothing can ever maul Christianity into oblivion.

The special interim report of Building Inspector 14759

A: PREFACE

It was deemed fit by the appropriate authorities, in the light of certain peculiar circumstances and the charges of some unnamed persons, that I, Building Inspector 14759, undertake to establish a commission of inquiry into the claims and activities of the said JESUS CHRIST.

Accordingly, I have done so, and have now completed the initial part of my investigations. Hereafter is my special interim report. Before concluding these few prefatory remarks, however, let me take the opportunity of sharing with you some anecdotal evidence which I believe will shed light on the information that follows. The subject of this investigation was the source of the anecdote.

> 'So then, anyone who hears these words of mine and obeys them is like a wise man who built his house on rock. The rain poured down, the rivers overflowed, and the wind blew hard against that house. But it did not fall, because it was built on rock.

> 'But everyone who hears these words of mine and does not obey them is like a foolish man who built his house on sand. The rain poured down, the rivers overflowed, the wind blew hard against that house, and it fell. And what a terrible fall that was!' (Matt. 7:24–27).

B: THE CHARGE

It has been charged by various persons that JESUS CHRIST is an unmitigated fraud, a fake who should be outlawed. They urge that people avoid him, and are intent on doing all within their power, using all the resources at their command, to secure his conviction and subsequent punishment. They advocate death.

As the basis for their accusations, these complainants use the following claim of JESUS CHRIST:

> 'Jesus answered, "Tear down this Temple, and in three days I will build it again."
> '"Are you going to build it again in three days?" they asked him. "It has taken forty-six years to build this Temple!"
> 'But the temple Jesus was speaking about was his body' (John 2:19-21).

It is interesting to note that the complainants include that last statement in their accusation; it is obvious that they do not understand its import.

C: THE EVIDENCE

I have spent a long time in a thorough search for proof of the charges made against JESUS CHRIST. The charges are most serious, and in the interests of justice I could afford to leave no stone unturned, no lead unfollowed. I have interviewed people, read documents, and gathered concrete evidence wherever possible.

I admit here and now that I approached this task quite cynically. I have dealt with the claims made by people who appeared like this JESUS CHRIST before, and it has always been my experience that those who preached the longest and the loudest, who made the greatest claims, had the least to offer. Instead, they would use all manner of falsehood, fast talking, and chicanery to deceive people so that they could achieve their own ends. Because of these experiences, I was quite prepared to find that none of the claims of JESUS CHRIST could be substantiated, and that the accusations would thus prove well-founded and the charges sustained.

The evidence I have uncovered points to a completely different conclusion. To ensure impartiality, and to allow you to take a balanced view of my recommendations, I intend to reproduce, immediately following, a summary of the information I have found. This information comes from those intimately acquainted with JESUS CHRIST, and includes quotes from an ancient and most authoritative source of knowledge.

(a) 'Come to the Lord, the living stone rejected by men as worthless, but chosen by God as valuable. Come as living stones, and let yourselves be used in building the spiritual temple, where you will serve as holy priests to offer spiritual and acceptable sacrifices to God through Jesus Christ. For the scripture says,
"I chose a valuable stone,
which I am placing as the cornerstone in Zion;
and whoever believes in him will never be disappointed".

This stone is of great value for you that believe; but for those who do not believe:
"The very stone which the builders rejected as worthless turned out to be the most important of all".

And another scripture says,
"This is the stone that will make people stumble, the rock that will make them fall".
They stumbled because they did not believe in the word; such was God's will for them' (1 Peter 2:4–8).

The following quotes reassert the points Peter has made:
(b) 'For God has already placed Jesus Christ as the one and only foundation, and no other foundation can be laid' (1 Cor. 3:11).

(c) 'But the solid foundation that God has laid cannot be shaken; and on it these words are written:
"The Lord knows those who are his" and "Whoever says that he belongs to the Lord must turn away from wrongdoing"' (2 Tim. 2:19).

(d) 'You, too, are built upon the foundation laid by the apostles and prophets, the cornerstone being Christ Jesus himself. He is the one who holds the whole building together and makes it grow into a sacred temple dedicated to the Lord. In union with him you too are being built together with all the others into a place where God lives through his Spirit' (Eph. 2:20-22).

D: THE CONCLUSION

You have now seen and read the same evidence that I have so far been presented with. You are therefore in a position to judge fairly the conclusions I draw about the claims of JESUS CHRIST.

My task was to discover whether or not JESUS CHRIST was guilty of being a fraud and thereby liable to punishment. On my investigations thus far, the only conclusion I can reasonably draw is that JESUS CHRIST is the true foundation of the saving of humanity. He is what he says. I would go so far as to say that there is no other on whom I would build my life. I am able to rest totally assured, and confident, in him. In light of the evidence I have presented, I believe there is no alternative, and that it could only be a stubborn fool who would attempt to find one.

I am aware that the time allocated to me to complete my investigations is not yet expired. Therefore, this can only be a special interim report. However, I am positive that the conclusions I draw here will prove to be the same conclusions that I draw when I present my final report, namely, that JESUS CHRIST is *not* a fake and *not* a fraud. I go further, and recommend that those who brought the charges against the accused be themselves subjected to the same rigorous investigation and questioning, so that their credibility and trustworthiness can be ascertained.

As it is, I conclude this special interim report with the proclamation that JESUS CHRIST is indeed true and faithful. He *is* the sure foundation!

E: FURTHER INFORMATION

If for any reason whatsoever, the evidence here presented is not sufficient for you to base a judgment on, I refer you to my primary source: the Bible.

Signed,

Building Inspector 14759

Falling in love again

Before you read any further than this paragraph, go to your record collection and pull out the album with your favourite love song on it. It should be soft and slow and warm, and it should make you feel like a melted chocolate inside. All right? Go and do it. . .

Took your time about it, didn't you?

I want you to relax into the song now. Let it flow around you, filling you up with all the memories it holds for you. Your eyes are getting misty and drifting far away. Time is slipping past; you're not feeling anything but the glow your first love brought you. Can you feel it? Has your tummy got up and flapped through the window on gossamer wings? Good — you're ready. For this is a story that needs that atmosphere; this is a story of love.

I fell in love for the first time at the age of thirteen. It happened just after my second major acne outbreak, and just before my first shave. It was as earth-shattering as both of those events.

Love sneaked up on me. I wasn't expecting it; I still 'hated' girls, and was still scared of their 'germs'. I was caught totally unawares. (I will not be tempted into using the cliché of 'being caught with my pants down'.)

There I was, strolling quite comfortably and quite confidently into teenagership, when it struck. 'It' was one of those sharp little arrows from chubby Cupid's bow. It came whistling through the air and pierced the armour of my young-man machismo.

I dismissed it first as growing pains — everything gets dismissed as growing pains at that age. Gradually, however, the symptoms began to sort themselves into some sort of pattern. They all seemed to occur because of a certain pretty young thing called . . . — it's probably safest not to mention her name.

Whenever I saw . . ., or even just thought about her, my stomach did flip-flops and my knees rattled. I'd grow weak and have to cling to door frames for support. And other strange things began to happen: I'd wash, put on clean shirts, demand that my pants be ironed. I got cravings for my father's after-shave. I even got to school *early*, just so I could be there to meet . . . when she arrived. This behaviour was so odd that my parents wanted to take me to the doctor.

That threat had no effect. I got worse. I took the unprecedented step of initiating conversation with a member of the opposite sex — without caring what my schoolmates said. I smiled at . . ., and punched her in the arm, and stole her pencil case and knocked her books on the floor just so I could pick them up, and offered her pieces of the chewing gum I was chewing by the truckload to keep my breath fresh.

Eventually, at a school dance, during the last dance, I asked her to be mine. She gripped my hand and said Yes, and I thought to myself: 'My goodness, isn't life just the most wonderful thing that could ever happen to a fellow!'

But alas, sometimes even fairytales have unhappy endings. Our 'love' did. It ended with my best friend's nose, which was little and cute, and . . . fell in love with it. I buried the sorrows of my pudgy nose in a hanky.

Of course, I've been in 'love' about a million times since then. I don't know what happens when you fall in love, whether some chemical reaction occurs or what, but I see that love still manages to be the subject of most of the songs in the Top 40 (although with a decidedly more sexual tilt than when I was a teenager).

When you love someone, you change.

The first thing that changes is the priority you give things. No longer do you rate yourself, and all your wants and wishes, as an automatic number one. You begin to think of the person you love. You try to do things that will make her (or him) happy — you buy flowers and chocolates, and put on good clothes — and you try very hard not to do anything that might hurt your friend.

You become like this, not because someone has laid down some law that you have to obey, but because you want to.

You don't do it because you think that it's the only way you'll keep your relationship intact: rather, it's something you just feel moved to do. It feels natural to want to make the other person happy. You hardly even know you're doing it. Making the other person happy makes you happy too.

This can lead you into doing things you'd never even dreamed of doing before: sitting through a four-hour opera, and then pretending you liked it; going to your friend's little sister's end-of-school concert, and joining in the singalongs; listening to the reminiscences of a forgetful old uncle, and assuring him that no, you weren't bored.

When you're in love, you want to spend as much time as you can with that person. You make time. Other things —even football — aren't as important any more.

As you get to know the person better, your relationship matures. You are able to share deeper, and even the deepest, things about yourself.

Inevitably, there come problems — there is no relationship without them. Maybe there is a nostalgic sadness for that first fresh-faced bloom of love. But you don't throw the whole relationship away because of a few problems (no matter how easy it has become these days). You work at your problems, you talk about them, you try to overcome them. You forgive. You say sorry. You compromise. This is the essence of a loving relationship.

It is the sort of relationship that we can share with God — because he has made us his special friends. This relationship is meant to grow and mature. One where we respond to God's Word and serve him — not because we have to, but because we want to. That is the test of the strength of our relationship with God — the way we respond to him, the degree to which our lives change to please him.

Our relationship with God is not a wimpoid, tacky, sloppy, B-grade movie one. It is strong and powerful, and it changes our lives. We become different people. God's love is perfect, and it can make up for the frailties of ours until we join God in his heaven. Our relationship, the love we can share, goes beyond death. And if you need any proof of the strength of God's love, if you don't believe me, you don't need to look any further than the battered and bloody body of God's Son hanging on the cross. That's what falling in love is all about.

72

Cigarettes

When I was 12, I never really believed that people my own age smoked. I realize things are different now, of course, that no sooner has a kid got the dummy out of its mouth than it has got a cigarette in it; but, back when I was 12, smoking seemed too enormous a thing even to contemplate.

Everyone talked about smoking. They brought along various evidences of their smoking — dead butts, empty packets, texta-coloured fingers, a fake cough — but none of it was convincing to me. I assumed only adults actually did smoke, and I felt quite safe in that.

Unfortunately, in the course of one too many lunchtime down-behind-the-gym sessions, I discovered that 12-year-olds *did* smoke. And to qualify as a fully paid-up member of the group, a 12-year-old *had* to smoke. Otherwise a 12-year-old wasn't normal.

This caused me great problems. No longer could I pretend to be a closet smoker; I would have to perform. I would actually have to stick that stinking burning thing into my mouth, and expertly exhale a cloud of blue smoke, hopefully in neat concentric circles, and do something called the drawback. What on earth was a drawback, besides a problem?

Rather than be embarrassed by a massive public failure, I decided I would have to practise. So it was that with a fearful heart and a great deal of knee clattering I entered that distant milk-bar (I couldn't go to the one nearby because I'd be recognized and reported to my parents) to buy my first packet of cigarettes. It was a pack of Escort 10s, and it cost 20 cents.

I tucked my illicit cargo down a football sock and sped on my pushbike as quickly as my legs would pedal me into the forest at the end of the road. There I found a large tree to sit behind, safe from any strolling and overly curious eyes.

Not having any smokers in my immediate family left me at a serious disadvantage. How did you smoke the things? The only thing I knew was that you didn't hold them in your hand, and try to light them there, a metre from your mouth (as a girl in our class had apparently done at a party).

Using my very basic knowledge of chemistry, I reasoned that for the end of the cigarette to glow (which seemed to be most of what smoking was all about), one would need to get oxygen going through it. Therefore I would have to *blow* oxygen through it.

I lit the cigarette and exhaled vigorously. Nothing happened. I lit the cigarette again, and exhaled even more vigorously. I exhaled until my ears stood out from my head and my eyes popped from their sockets. Still nothing. I tried a different cigarette. The same result. And another. Again. It was just my luck, I grumbled to myself, that I'd get a packet of brummy cigarettes.

Eventually, completely accidentally, I inhaled. And for a brief second I saw the end of the cigarette glow. But only for a second. In the next instant, smoke filled my lungs, tears filled my eyes, and I felt as if I was dying.

When the smoke cleared, and when I had fully recovered from the fit of coughing that had shaken me like a kid shakes a rag doll, I attempted again what I had just achieved. I inhaled, I saw the end of the cigarette glow, and I tried to convince myself that I was enjoying a wonderful and deeply significant experience.

From that time on, I carefully exposed a cigarette packet whenever and wherever possible — in the school locker rooms, on geography excursions, at teenage parties. My big mistake, however, was smoking menthol cigarettes. I did not realize that real men smoked only certain brands, brands that had a lot to do with cowboy hats and horses. Now that I come to think of it, the taste of those cigarettes had something about it reminiscent of horses.

So, smoking became a habit. I don't think I ever really enjoyed the burning thing at the end of my fingers then, but I pretended I did. Except for the time I lit a Winfield after the inter-school cross-country in which I'd walked a mediocre

Losefield* 25s
Losefield* 25s

second last. I'm not real good with colours, so I don't know if what my friends said was true or not, but they reckoned lime green was not a tint that suited my particular style of facial feature. I was in no position to comment, being doubled-up over my drastically distorted internal organs.

I have since given up smoking cigarettes, and have transferred my allegiance to a theoretically once-a-day pipe. It seems that many others too are 'swearing off the gaspers', with the encouragement of governments and health authorities. The only problem is that if everyone stops smoking, who is going to sponsor all the sport in Australia?

It is very easy for your whole life to develop along the lines down which smoking led me. What we choose to do may really be chosen for us by the attitudes of the world and the people important to us. We can fall into doing only what they tell us we ought to be doing. They can be so persuasive that we can forget that we have a mind of our own, and put ourselves through horrors just so that we can be like them, merging into an anonymous mindless background. And, sooner than we realize, it becomes a habit.

We don't think about it any more, and we find we've come so far that there is no turning back, that we can't give it up — that we don't even want to give it up.

I reckon we all have to take a look at ourselves, and the sort of life we're living, and ask just how come we've decided to live our life this way. Is it just a habit we've fallen into because the pressures of the world around us make it more comfortable this way? Are we conforming to the ways of the world just for the approval of the world? It's terribly easy to go along with what everyone else is doing, without ever calling a halt and just asking why.

Paul says:
> 'Do not conform yourselves to the standards of this world, but let God transform you inwardly by a complete change of mind. Then you will be able to know the will of God — what is good and is pleasing to him and is perfect' (Rom. 12:2).

Which sounds pretty good advice to me.

I told you this story about me and cigarettes not to say that a good Christian shouldn't smoke, or to try to persuade you all to give up smoking — that's your decision. I just wanted to show that we have to be careful not to conform to the ways of the world. The reasons are in that verse from Romans. And while we're at it, that sort of thinking can help us to avoid the trap of routine religion, too. Think about it.

God has given us brains, and he's given us the gift of freedom of choice. Most of all, he's given us his Spirit. Let's use these gifts.

The case for the defence

Note from the Court Reporter:

Herewith please find the official court transcript of the summing up for the Defence by the Defence Counsellor (acting for himself) in the trial by Judge alone in the case of the Crown versus the Defence, wherein it is alleged that the Defendant did, continually and irrevocably, and with malice aforethought, fail most grievously to perform the duty he willingly sustained when he entered, completely voluntarily, into the agreement in another place detailed. That is, he failed to witness to the faith he professed.

The Defence:

Your . . . er . . .Honour . . . er . . . Your Worship . . . and . . . er . . . ladies and gentlemen.

I . . . um . . . wish to sum up the case for the defence by . . . um . . . appealing to your knowledge of the world, to your ability to think clearly, to your facility for seeing things as they really are. When you *do* see things as they really are, then I trust you will reach the appropriate verdict. I mean, the verdict that goes my way.

I realize that, at first glance, and perhaps second and third glance too, it might appear that I did, well, more accurately, didn't, do what this case is all about, that is, witness to the faith I profess. And I do profess it, I assure you. But, BUT, I urge you, I implore you, I beg you, to look deeper, to look beyond the facts. There are extenuating circumstances, reasons, for my actions, er, my lack of action. In other words, take it easy on me.

The extenuating circumstances with which I want to acquaint you are as follows. There are lots of them, and I would ask you to pay very close attention:

78

1. I am shy. I blush even to say it. I don't find it easy to talk to people. Old people or new people. About anything. Weather or football or politics or pop groups. Anything —let alone God. I can't help it. It's not my fault. It's hereditary. Shyness runs in our family. None of our family are great talkers. Well, none of the male members of our family are great talkers. I don't know why. It just happens. I freeze up. And I stammer. I mean I s . . . s . . . st . . .st . . . sta . . . sta . . . stamm . . . stamm . . . stammer . . .er . . . er.

2. I don't know if you realize it or not, but God is no longer an appropriate topic of conversation. God is out of fashion. People just don't talk about God any more. They have more important — whoops! I didn't mean that, Your Honour, it just slipped out. Things-slipping-out runs in our family, too, Your Worship. What I meant was that people have different things to talk about these days. Like their new hairstyles, and like their best friend's husband's habit of picking his teeth in public, and sex sex sex, and the future as we know it, and big bombs, and lots of things like that. Everything —well, everything except God. It's not my fault that it's not polite to talk about God in public.

3. No one believes in God any more, anyway. The scientists say they've proved that God doesn't exist with molecules and computers and uranium. You can't argue with them. Or maybe *you* could — you're brainy. But I'm not. I don't have enough brilliant arguments to counter all theirs. It's not that I don't want to, heaven forbid — um, no disrespect intended — it's that I can't. If I had a degree in theology, I would. Or if I could read Ancient Greek. But I can't, so I don't and I won't.

4. Now that they've stopped believing in God, people have got new gods, and they talk about them. So I have to be polite and join in. I know a lot about jogging, and low-fat ice-cream, and leotards.

5. Besides, I really don't think it is fair of me to try to force my opinions on someone else. Everyone has the right to believe what they like, without always having someone jumping up and down in front of them telling them what they should do and think. That's a fundamental right, and I hold a high moral position about it. Each to his or her own, I say. Don't Bible bash!

Interjection from Prosecutor:

Objection, Your Honour. I submit that everyone and everything else in the world insists on having its say without interruption, and that the Christian is entitled to his or her say, too.

Judge:

Objection sustained.

Defence:

If you please, Your Honour. I was just trying to do my part, to set a good example. I thought that if I didn't witness, people might get the idea, and not try to indoctrinate me with their views. But, let me go on.

6. Why should *I* witness? We've got professionals to do it for us. There are missionaries and preachers and people on TV and volunteers — they're enthusiastic and they get paid for it. It's *their* job, not mine.

7. And even so, I *do* help. I donate money. *And* I've got a bumper sticker of a fish on my car, and we all know what *that* means.

Interjection from Prosecutor:

Objection, Your Honour. The fish the Defence Counsellor refers to is nothing more than a drawing of a shark holding a bedraggled fisherman in its jaws, with the caption: 'I got caught in Mallacoota'.

Judge:

Is that true?

Defence:

Yes, but it's the thought that . . .

Judge:

Objection sustained. Now continue, and stick to the truth.

Defence:

8. Perhaps you don't know, Your Honour, but the only people that witness these days are the weirdo religious groups, the ones in the suits and ties and name-tags going from door to door. I wouldn't want to be confused with them. Everyone knows that they take the whole thing too seriously, giving up their free time, being brave enough to knock on people's door and having the dog sooled on them, giving witnessing a bad name.

9. I'm a busy person. I've got lots of things to do, a whole life to run. I just don't have the time to be an effective witness, or any sort of witness at all. If I had more time, I would. I could, I'm sure I could. And would.

10. Finally, the tenth reason is that — I don't know the best way to put this, so you'll forgive me if I do it badly — God doesn't suit my new image, my racy person-about-the-place look. He just doesn't match. If God could update a bit — not necessarily go punk, but just ease up a bit — things would be much easier and there would be no problem. The trouble is, the way God looks now, well, he's a bit of an ... embarrassment.

To sum up, it is just too hard to stand up and actually admit that you are a Christian. There are too many reasons not to. And if you can't admit that, then no one can expect you to witness to your faith, to share it, by actually going up to other real-life people and telling them about it. The idea is ludicrous.

It is much more sensible to do as I have done. To be inoffensive, to avoid causing trouble, to be careful not to disrupt, let alone confront, anyone. I have been a ... quiet ... yes, quiet ..., witness.

Note from the Court Reporter:

It was at that point that the Defence Counsellor retired, and rested his case. The Prosecutor then arose, and his only act was to quote a precedent from the law:
> 'If a person is ashamed of me and of my teaching in this godless and wicked day, then the Son of Man will be ashamed of him when he comes in the glory of his Father with the holy angels' (Mark 8:38).

Upon this, the Prosecutor rested his case.

The Judge found the charge proved.

Words are not enough

As I write these words, I am sitting in a library. It is not the largest library in the world. In fact, I suppose it is quite small, and relatively insignificant, even on a State-wide scale, let alone national or international.

Yet, limited though it is, this library contains tens of thousands of books. They stretch, row after row after row, across the air-conditioned plushly-carpeted hush-hush room that holds them.

There is a seemingly endless variety of books here. There are big glossy coloured picture books, and there are battered old books with yellowing pages. There are ancient books and brand new books. There are popular books and famous books; and there are obscure and rarely-read books.

There are books that address the question of existence as a whole, that look at everything in a sweeping overview and try to make sense of it. There are other books that take the tiniest fraction of one particular facet from just one small area of life and examine it in the minutest detail.

There are books from every discipline: history, art, religion, philosophy, mathematics, drama, music, language, research data, et cetera, et cetera, et cetera.

All of these books are listed on a microfiche catalogue. There, on a little piece of plastic, which suddenly becomes huge and comprehensible when placed under a magnifier, are all the details of the book. There is the title, the author, the number of pages, the place of publication, a description of the contents — you almost expect to find what mood the author was in when the book was written. The most important information — for the reader, anyway — is the location of the book in the library.

There, on this one small piece of plastic, on this fraction of this one small piece of plastic, is the key to that part of the sum of human knowledge that is contained in just one book in just one library of all the libraries of the world.

Into this library I plunged. I searched for knowledge in what seemed an endless array of books. I could not count the books, let alone the chapters, the pages, the words.

How many words have we human beings written?

The number seems infinite, though I know from Grade 6 Maths that it's not.

How many are the ideas that we have sweated from our souls, stolen from our experience, conjured from the depths of our rationality?

Human beings have worked long and hard in an effort to take a firm hand-hold on the meaning of their existence. They've tried to catalogue it, to summarize it in easily-accessible form. They've tried to write the explanation for the life that pushes their bodies until death. How many sacrifices human beings have made on the altar of knowledge to try to gain the final answer to their ultimate question: Why? How many more will they make?

No matter what the number of words is that has been written, and no matter how many more will be added to that store, and no matter how brilliant the computer that can be constructed becomes, the question will always remain: Why? We are no closer to unlocking the door to this knowledge than we ever were. This knowledge remains safe and secure from our prying type of learning.

All our words pass away. Their life is nothing more than a mid-summer fancy. The source of life that they have tried to explain remains hidden. Our millions of millions of words can never bring it to light, and that might lead us to identify with the resigned words of the writer of Ecclesiastes, who says:
> 'My son, there is something else to watch out for. There is no end to the writing of books, and too much study will wear you out' (Eccl. 12:12).

Frustrated in its search for ultimate answers, humanity can become alienated and depressed. It can try to create an answer for itself by fashioning one out of the dust of the earth, by melting down all its gold and jewellery to produce its own golden calf.

This is a futile pastime. The answer already exists. It has always existed. Not in millions of words, but in one word. *The* Word.

> 'Before the world was created, the Word already existed; he was with God, and he was the same as God. From the very beginning the Word was with God. Through him God made all things; not one thing in all creation was made without him. The Word was the source of life, and this life brought light to mankind. The light shines in the darkness, and the darkness has never put it out' (John 1:1-5).

This is the Word, the Word who became a human being (John 1:14). We need only believe on it, on him.

And God has made it easy for us. He has expanded this Word into one book, the Bible, so that we can read and understand the message given to us. God has put all that we need to know into the Bible. The Word which is the Bible points us to the Word who is Jesus Christ. There is more that could be known, but all that is important to us is here. When John concludes his gospel, he notes:

> 'Now, there are many other things that Jesus did. If they were all written down one by one, I suppose that the whole world could not hold the books that would be written' (John 21:25).

That is the richness of the one Word we have been given. The final, the essential, the only necessary Word in all the books of all the libraries in all of time. Thank God it has been given to us.

A² = B² + C²
TEAC
Teacher.
KUNG FU

To sir with love

'To sir with love.'

That was what was written on the paper dart that collided with my nose, doing some nasty damage to it. The paper dart was followed by various other projectiles, at various speeds. In the barrage, I detected chalk, screwed-up paper, history books, and abuse.

The reason for this warfare was that I was unfortunate enough to be asked to do a stint of relief teaching. It is called 'relief teaching', but a more accurate description would be 'monster-sitting'. After dodging projectiles, trying to forestall full-scale riots, and just generally weighing the value of my life, I can understand why relief teachers are required.

It wouldn't have been so bad if I could have had the benefit of a few teacher's aids — a machine-gun, a few hand-grenades, and a stock of napalm — but I didn't.

The thing about relief teachers — at least the inexperienced brand that I was — is that they don't really have any authority. They hand out work, and tell students to be quiet. If the students choose not to be quiet, if they choose to break each others' arms and legs, if they choose to do some of the other smelly things that lively young students do, there is not a real lot the relief teacher can do. I yelled: 'QUIET!' And for a split second, I'm sure, the noise stopped. It was just an instant, no longer than the time it takes to blink, but it *did* stop.

However, there is only a limited number of times that a relief teacher can yell 'QUIET' before it loses its shock value, or before the relief teacher's voice fades to a croak. If the riot continues, what else is there to do? Send the whole class out of the room? Run crying to the Head? Call out the local SWAT team?

There is a question of authority involved, and whether or not the relief teacher has any. Students don't think so, and can perceive no threat potent enough to make them turn from their relief-teacher-destroying ways. And I can't really blame them — I probably did the same thing when I was at school. The destruction of a teacher, real or relief, is notched up as a victory. Students collect them like wartime fighter pilots collected enemy planes, marking their victims down on their fuselage.

What it all comes down to is that there are two ways to try to get people to do what you want them to do. The first is to have a big stick — it might be violence or blackmail or the threat of failure — and to wield it. If the stick is big enough, you'll get your way.

The other method is to present to people what you want them to do, explain why, and then leave it up to them to decide whether or not they'll do it.

When I was under siege in that classroom, dreaming of a chattering M16, I was looking to the first method. However, I was only able to use the second method, because they don't sell machine-guns to teachers any more. (There were fears that the breed of student would become extinct.) The second method is frustrating, depressing, nerve-tearing — and I couldn't bear it.

If you look at the way God worked in the Old Testament with the Israelites, it sometimes seems as if he used a pretty big stick. First of all, there was the power he showed by the things he did to the Egyptians — the ten plagues, the Red Sea swimming lessons, and so on. You reckon this would show the Israelites that here was a God with power, with power enough to demand whatever he wants, and to get it.

The Israelites don't seem to have had more than a few grams of brain between them — or, if they did, then their memories were short. Because over and over and over again, they forgot about God and went and did their own thing. So God punished them — allowed them to be decimated in battle (Num. 14:45), sent snakes to bite them (Num 21:6), and prohibited them from entering the Promised Land for 40 years. What we see is God using the big-stick approach.

If God wanted to, he could club all of *us* over the head too, with the reality of his presence and his holiness. He could make it so that we had no option but to do what he demanded. But God gives us a choice. He calls us, and draws us to believe in him and to accept his love and forgiveness, but we can still be stupid and pig-headed, and reject him.

The wonderful thing about God giving us this choice is that it recognizes our individuality, our personhood, and our capacity to make decisions. It gives us worth, allows us to be more than puppets or pre-programmed robots.

Therefore, when we *do* come into a relationship with God, we come into a loving father-child relationship, and not that of a master and slave. Surely the first is infinitely better. (Even with the Israelites, God tried hard to establish a loving father-child relationship.)

I spent one short day in a classroom, and I was ready to tear all my hair out. There is probably nothing more nerve-jangling than watching people with a choice make the wrong one, to go off and have what seems, at that moment, like 'a real good time'. There will come a time when every one of those people will realize the mistake they have made, and the opportunity they have wasted.

God's position in relation to us is much more difficult than was mine in relation to those students. God loves us and cares for us, and it must hurt him really badly to see us going astray. If you or I were in that situation, we would want to yank us up by the hair and to shake our feeble bodies until they get some sense back into them.

I thank God that he doesn't force us to do what he wants. I thank him for the love he freely gives, and also for the choice he gives to me and to every one of us individually. I pray we choose wisely. (If *you* don't, I'll send one of the boys round to thump you until you do!)

Waiting for the zed

There's a young man standing on the roof of a shopping centre where young couples are buying things to fill up new homes. The young man is standing on the roof of the shopping centre, pointing a gun into the sky.

(When it was all over, they said he'd been there all afternoon, pacing up and down the roof — no one had noticed him. He had provisions and music. Well-prepared. And the coroner said it was a scene from *Macbeth*.)

He's pointing a gun into the sky, and he's looking out into the distance, to a place somewhere far beyond the edge of sky that comes creeping in behind his eyes. He's looking into the distance and waiting. Waiting for the zed.

I've got his picture here, right alongside me, so I can tell the truth. I'm typing as I'm staring. The picture was in the morning paper, 14.4 centimetres high — I measured it. High on the roof of a shopping centre. Pointing a gun into the sky. Staring out from behind daring eyes. Eyes daring to be nothing.

Last night, when it was happening, there were news-flashes all the time. Very regular — like ads. But they weren't ads; they came between the soaps, the operas, and ads. Right to the end — when he blew his brains out. Nice and graphic. Great front-page spread. Always works better when they're dead. Waiting for the zed.

    A. The doctor's got a white mask and a knife. He hit me.

    B. Someone's splashing water on my head. It's cold.

    C. Walking, talking.

    D. Mother, mother, mother, mother, mother, mother.

E. Fell in love with someone bigger than me. Pulled my hair.

F. Didn't love . . . any more.

G. Old enough to watch a grandparent die.

H. Young enough to cry.

I. I'm a teenager now, but I'll soon be adult. I'm running away from these days because they're too loud. Too close. I'm running away, looking for tomorrow, a tomorrow for me. I'm waiting.

J. Tomorrow.

K. Today. I think. Not running any more. Standing still. Lying down. Waiting. Waiting curled up in a ball. Waiting for the zed.

It can sneak up on you, or be hiding behind doors you've opened a million times before. It can be waiting where there have only ever been smiles. It can tiptoe in, in socks, or bellow a million car-crashes before its time. But it's there.

Waiting for the zed; the zed waits for no one.

They wrote down three-score-and-ten to use as an average. It's a mark on a wall for you to stand up against. You don't grow, the mark descends. It's an average, but an agony if there's a cancer creeping through your flesh. And it's an average too small if you're lovely, loving, or loved.

A real average is maybe 64.3 for males and more if you're blushing feminine. And it's a number that will never be average again, after it's been average accurate for you. It's never average being hit, being hit around, being hit down, being zed.

Big brave men strutting around Westerns, packing six-shooters, are never scared. They fall from their horses and eat dust and spill tomato sauce and grunt and lie still after a few seconds, but they don't flinch. They don't feel the iron muscle of zed flexing a second below each passing breath. They don't smell the rot and the flowers and the tears.

I can say I'm not scared. Be brave, young person, be brave. I could pretend to hope. I could climb up on top of a shopping centre and be a young man waiting. Waiting quietly with music and provisions, and with a girlfriend that the authorities couldn't find until it was too late, for any sense to be talked through my head. I could telephone the uniforms down on the ground and invite ladders and comfort and only be tricking, but I'd still just be waiting. Each second of wait just a little shorter, each next step just a little more uncertain.

Can't scare it away!

Can't say: Leave me alone, I'm not waiting for you!

Can't say: Don't want you, want to be on my own. Holy words and holy prayers and curses and heroin and a million lovers and a million dollars don't scare you. You're inevitable. Can't move you one position further on. You're at the end, you *are* the end. And I'm just waiting. You come when you come, and I can't know. A screaming jet from the sky, and a parachute that won't open, and, in those last few seconds of falling, feeling the ground rushing up to greet me with its open arms and its cavity excavated just for me, and being able to do nothing but wait wait wait — waiting for the zed.

> '"Listen!" says Jesus. "I am coming soon! I will bring my rewards with me, to give to each one according to what he has done. I am the first and the last, the beginning and the end" ' (Rev. 22:12,13).

The Alpha and the Omega. The first and the last. The beginning and the end. The A and the Zed. Waiting for the zed. I can only say Amen: Yea, yea, it shall be so. I'm waiting for the zed; beyond zed, You're waiting for me. Amen. Amen. Amen.

Down on the farm

When I was a little bloke, our family used to spend the school holidays down on the farm. (Both Mum and Dad grew up on farms, so we even had a choice.)

Farms are great places. They are full of interesting things to do, things you can't do in the city. It's amazing the freedom a few hundred or a few thousand acres gives you; sunrise to sunset isn't long enough to fit it all in.

You can go up to the scrub with a spade that's twice as big as you are, and dig a hole. You can make a roof out of sticks and leaves, and call it a fort. You can stock it with old cans and the bleached white bones of sheep, and hide in it. You can hope that your big nasty cousin doesn't sneak up behind you and throw half-a-dozen penny-bungers inside.

You can go to the yards outside the shearing shed and drag half a gum tree around behind you, pretending you're doing the cultivating. Or you can gather a cousin, or brother or two, and produce a mob of sheep. You do this by crawling around underneath the shearing shed, knee deep in mean-and-nasties, baaing for all you're worth. You know you've been successful when Nana comes racing out of the kitchen, still up to the elbows in flour, to see what mob 'Dad' has brought home now.

On a farm, you can make a track through the grass that springs up green and fresh after the rain. You stamp the track down with your feet; you put in a few 'straights', an S-bend or two, and various other twists and turns, and perhaps a jump. Then you run along it as fast as you can, spinning out a few times, pretending you're a racing-car driver.

Most farms have haystacks, and they're put there specially for kids from the city to crawl into. You can have a mighty game of hide-and-seek in a haystack; and if you get sick of that, you can play another game that involves seeing who can dong the most mice on the head with a bit of wood in a set time.

And so the days on the farm used to pass. By the time the sun has set, even the healthiest kid would be exhausted, filthy, and so hungry that he could eat a whole frying-pan-full of Nana's sausages and gravy, and still feel he had cause enough to start a brawl over who would get the crust from the fresh white bread.

The only trouble used to be that, before you could get inside to the food, you had to get cleaned up. No kid likes getting cleaned up, and I wasn't one to be an exception to the rule. I didn't see anything wrong with cowdung on my boots and grass-stains on my knees, or with burrs in my hair and blood on my nose. It's only adults who get fussed about that sort of thing.

What happened to us because of that fussing was that we'd get thrown into a steaming bath and told to get clean. Everyone knows it is impossible for a kid to get clean without making some pretty big splashes, so I don't know why Dad got so cross when he waded in.

He'd stand there in gum boots and raincoat and give orders, distributing soap and scrubbing brushes left, right, and centre. I am sure the scrubbing brushes were made out of fencing wire and used for stripping paint when they weren't being used to scrub kids' knees and elbows.

When we thought we were near enough to being clean, we'd present ourselves for inspection. Dad would look behind our ears, and always make the same crack about there being enough dirt there to grow potatoes. We'd have to get rid of that before we were allowed out of the bathroom (which was on the back verandah) and into the house.

We got rid of the dirt, towelled off, and then puffed enough baby powder around the bathroom to make porridge out of the water on the floor. Then we'd jump into our warm flannelette pyjamas, slippers, and dressing gowns. And inside to a huge tea, the ABC news and weather, and finally a crispy crunchy clean bed. Paradise!

Those days down on the farm are a long time ago now; but though the memories are distant, they still leave a warm impression. That impression, for me, approximates what heaven is like — sort of warm, sort of cosy, sort of comfortable.

And just as I couldn't get into the farm house until I was washed clean, I can't enter heaven until the grubbiness of my sin has been washed away. I could try to do that myself, but I'd never succeed, so God has given us Christ to do the job for us. That's what his dying on the cross, and resurrection, was for.

Sometimes it is a bit hard to understand why, if God is such a loving and merciful God, he doesn't just let everyone come to live in heaven with him as they are. When I think about those days down on the farm, I think I begin to understand why. If we had gone inside when we were dirty, we would have messed the place up. It wouldn't have been nice for us for very long, and it would have spoiled it for everyone else. At the time, it might have seemed easier and kinder for me to be let inside just how I was, but it wasn't until I was clean that I could really appreciate it.

The same applies to heaven. For it to stay the perfect place it is, it has to be kept free of the contamination of sin. God has set things up so that we *can* be freed from sin, and so be free to enter heaven perfectly. We only have to be washed clean by Christ, in whose blood our sins are forgiven.

Listen to these words from one of the Psalms:
    'Remove my sin, and I will be clean;
    wash me, and I will be whiter than snow' (Ps. 51:7).
And hear what John writes about forgiveness:
    'If we say that we have no sin, we deceive ourselves,
    and there is no truth in us. But if we confess our sins to
    God, he will keep his promise and do what is right: he
    will forgive us our sins and purify us from all our
    wrongdoing' (1 John 1:8,9).

That is all there is to it.

The memory of the happiness of those days down on the farm remains clear, despite the passing of time. In the same way, but in the opposite direction, I think of heaven. I look forward to it. It seems far away, and maybe a lot will happen to me before then, but I feel as if I have a foretaste of it in my memory of the days I spent down on the farm.

OxFORD
Dictionary

Peripatetic

Peripatetic: what a great word! It's got a nice ring to it, hasn't it? It runs off the tongue with a rattle like a machine gun: Peripatetic.

I've just discovered it, actually. Just think, I've been wandering about this earth for 25 years, and until today I'd never seen a peripatetic. So, naturally, when it confronted me, I got a bit of a fright. I didn't recognize it. I came to a screaming halt, took a quick look, then fled.

But I had to come back the same way to get through the article I was reading. And there it was again. It had not moved. I looked at it. It looked back — beadily. I side-stepped. It side-stepped — quicker. I tried to say it. My tongue got caught on the second-last of the five syllables and came a nasty cropper.

Well, I couldn't let that pass without some sort of masculine response. 'All right, you dirty low-down rat of a peripatetic', I hissed, 'You asked for it! I'm getting out the Concise Oxford'. My hand shot to my dictionary before the peripatetic could move. You should have seen that word cringe — it knew its game was up. It knew I was going to discover its meaning, its origin, and even its pronunciation.

I looked it up. Well, I never — who would have guessed it meant that? Peripatetic: . . I won't tell you just yet what it means: it could be dangerous if the peripatetic is still listening.

Anyway, I took that meaning, and I inserted it back into the sentence from which I'd extracted the peripatetic — and, do you know, it fitted perfectly. It made sense.

Absolutely thrilled with myself, I practised my brilliant new word over a number of times just to get the pronunciation right. Then I tried it in a few sentences, just so I could feel at home with it. Soon I was able to whip it out and use it as easily as I could a word like peripeteia.

Now that I had my new word perfect, I did with it what anyone else would do — I showed off. You know what it's like. You engage some friends in what they think is a casual conversation, lulling them into a false sense of security, but all the time you're gradually steering the talk toward a point where your new word will be relevant.

So, for peripatetic, I started telling a joke about a guy who goes from door to door selling vacuum cleaners. I could have talked about the Pope. Then, when I was ready, I fired away with peripatetic.

It's interesting watching people's reactions to a word most of them have probably never heard before. Do they pretend they know what it means? Do they anxiously try to work out its meaning from its context? Do they ignore it? Do they change the subject? Disagree vehemently? Say 'Pardon?'? Or do they feel sure enough of themselves to ask what the word means?

And what about *you*? If I called you peripatetic, would you give me a clout round the ear-hole, feel flattered, ask how I knew that about you, or just wonder why on earth I used the word in that context? Well, *you* mightn't be peripatetic, but I'm pretty sure the jolly swagman was.

The funny thing about discovering a new word is that, no sooner have you learnt what it means, you see the word all over the place, three or four times in the first week, even though before then you had never even heard of it. Is this just coincidence, or has the word always been there, but you failed to recognize it?

When you run into the Bible for the first time, or the first time for a while, you'll most likely come to a pretty sudden stop. And maybe you'll hang a squealing U-ie and disappear in the other direction. I suppose that is understandable —the Bible's a heavy book, both in size and content. But, what do you do with something heavy? Ignore it and hope it goes away?

Or maybe you'll stick your nose inside this book and take a look. You may be able to read the words, but you may not know what they mean, so you try substituting a whole cluster of approximate meanings, and hope that, together, they get pretty close to the original. Instead of going deep into God's Word to find out what he is actually saying to us, we may just stick to a few fairly easy things and hope that they'll get us by.

Or maybe you'll go for Bible substitutes, ones that are easier to read — books like this one. That's all right if you realize that they *aren't* substitutes for the Bible, that they're just helpers. This book is written in the hope that it will stir you up enough to go and read the original, to find out what God is saying there.

Let's go back to the Bible, and see what God tells us about his Word.

> 'Heaven and earth will pass away, but my words will never pass away' (Matt. 24:35).

> 'But as for you, continue in the truths that you were taught and firmly believe. You know who your teachers were, and you remember that ever since you were a child, you have known the Holy Scriptures, which are able to give you the wisdom that leads to salvation through faith in Christ Jesus. All Scripture is inspired by God and is useful for teaching the truth, rebuking error, correcting faults, and giving instruction for right living, so that the person who serves God may be fully qualified and equipped to do every kind of good deed' (2 Tim. 3:14-17).

> 'Your word is a lamp to guide me
> and a light for my path' (Ps. 119:105).

There are some pretty good reasons to read God's Word among that lot — and they should be encouragement enough for anybody.

An interesting thing you'll find when you read the Bible is that what you read is relevant to what is happening in your life at that moment. You'll recognize God's message to you in a whole lot of unexpected places. Just as after learning a new word you seem to see it everywhere, so with God's Word. That's a blessing he gives us.

Well, what are you waiting for? I'm finished. Go and get on with your reading!

Peripatetic?

Haven't I given you the meaning yet? Sorry, I thought I had. Peripatetic means . . . — O, don't be so lazy; go and look it up for yourself! You'll remember it much better then.

Uncle Ross

My Dad's parents were practically German, and lived in a place so tiny it didn't have a pub, called Milendella. We used to go and visit them; and to the little boy I was then, it always seemed to be hot and dusty. I think they had a drought every year.

Time has a way of punching everything out of focus, and details become just an impression. I'm not sure, but I think my Uncle Ross lived with my grandparents. What I am sure of is the horror I felt when once I watched Uncle Ross (a butcher) slaughter a sheep, only to find him chasing me with its stomach and telling me it was what sausage skins were made from.

One holiday when we were down at Milendella, Uncle Ross took my brother and sister and me for a ride in his panel van. That was way back in the times when panel vans were work vehicles rather than playpens. He sped us along a bumpy dusty road, and us kids bounced around the back having a great time. After a while, he began singing/shouting a song, and he taught it is us. It was called 'Yakkity Yak Blah Blah Blah Blah'. It doesn't have a lot of words besides those of the title, but it's a great song.

All of a sudden, Uncle Ross told us to quick look out of the window because there was an elephant on the side of the road. Of course, we jumped out of our skins and had a major brawl to get to the window first to see the elephant. We were very disappointed when we couldn't spot it. Uncle Ross just said: 'O, you missed it'.

We'd only been sitting down a few minutes when Uncle Ross saw another elephant. We missed that one, too. Then he saw a zebra and a hippopotamus. It was only when he got to the purple-bellied tree-climbing people-eating rock-hopping bongo monster that we realized we were being tricked.

I was always a bit scared of Uncle Ross. He had a bit of an accent, and I couldn't always understand what he said. And he swore quite a bit, and smoked cigarettes, and his clothes always seemed to be dirty, and he drank beer, but he always treated us kids as if we were adult and important.

Times change and people grow older, and they grow apart. My grandparents died, and our family moved interstate, and Milendella and Uncle Ross seemed too far away for us to get there very often any more.

At one time, Uncle Ross got very sick, and went to hospital. He was Dad's big brother, and my godfather, and Dad and I went to visit him. He was at the end of a long sickly-clean corridor, lying very quietly between starched white sheets. His eyes were open, but he didn't seem to see us. My Dad said he didn't know who we were. I didn't understand how that could be — Uncle Ross knew who I was: I was Jonathan, his godson.

Uncle Ross got better, but we were far away. Us kids still occasionally sang 'Yakkity Yak', and my brother developed a brilliance at convincing unsuspecting people that they'd just missed seeing an elephant.

On my twenty-second birthday, Uncle Ross died. Something to do with a blood clot. My Dad and I went to the funeral, and we sat right up near the front. The coffin looked very big so close up, and as I stared at it I recalled the few glimpses of Uncle Ross I had that created the person I remember him as. I hadn't known him well, or closely. I had been scared of him. Yet, there was something, something I couldn't define, that bonded us. Maybe it was the ties of blood, or the fact that Uncle Ross was my sponsor. Whatever it was, I felt some kinship. And as the minister said the parting words over Harold Ross Krause, I thought about what that kinship meant.

It seems that we never get to know anyone as well as we could, not even our family or the person we marry. There always seems to be something deeper that we can't touch, and can't articulate, and can't explain. It is as if, deep within, we have the potential for a wonderful, perfect relationship, which at times we gain glimpses of. At the death of someone close, in the stillness that comes after the shock, we may feel that hint of relationship more strongly. The hollowness we feel says that the sleeping person is someone close.

It is this feeling of kinship, friendship, and fellowship that we can only glimpse now, which Christ perfects in his resurrection. When we join together in heaven as Christians, the barriers that separate us here — the things that, while making each of us the person we are, at the same time distance us from one another — will fall away. Freed of our earthly shackles, we will have perfect communion with each other, as well as with God. That's an incredible thought. Paul writes about it in Romans:

> 'We have many parts in the one body, and all these parts have different functions. In the same way, though we are many, we are one body in union with Christ, and we are all joined to each other as different parts of one body' (Rom. 12:4,5).

If we can take into our daily lives some of that love and kinship and unity which we have because of Christ, maybe we can experience more of the joy of heaven here on earth, and maybe we can spread a little more love about this hurting and grieving world.

When the funeral service for Uncle Ross finished, we came out and shook hands with people we hadn't seen for years. Then we got into our cars and followed the hearse down the bumpy dusty road to the cemetery.

The funeral procession had to stop because two cows wandered out on to the road. They made me smile, because I thought Uncle Ross would have appreciated that. There were two animals that I hadn't 'missed'.

The art of keeping animals in cages outside the zoo

(an interview with the Keeper of the Cage)

You'd like to learn the art of keeping animals in cages outside the zoo? Certainly. It is quite simple. But first let me acquaint you with the circumstances which made the genesis of such an art imperative.

What happened was very strange, but the day that led up to it was in no way unusual. In fact, it was quite quiet —perhaps we should have suspected something when it was that quiet.

The animals had just been fed — when I say fed, I mean they had been thrown their few scraps of sustenance, just enough to keep them alive — and had lain down and fallen into their usual state: slumber. A few visitors gawked — more out of surprise that the animals still existed than out of curiosity — and a few young ones threw rocks, but there were no other signs of movement. So, as anyone else would naturally do, we keepers put our feet up and watched sport on TV.

There was no warning for what happened next. We first knew that something was wrong when the noise started. There was trumpeting and thundering and the clashing of metal on metal. It was a fearful cacophany, and our first thoughts were of war; but when we looked out of the window, we saw what was really happening, and we were astounded.

As I said before, the usual state of the animals is slumber, but something had changed all that now. It was as if some spark, some spirit, had come down from out of the blue and taken hold of the animals, set fire to them. Totally roused from their melancholy and their drowsiness, they were so alive that they seemed to burst from their skins.

Before we could do anything — even just getting out the fire hoses and dousing them with cold water — they exploded out of the cold stone walls that contained them. They broke down the heavy wooden doors, burst out of their cages, and helped one another to escape out into the world.

It is a disaster of the greatest dimension. Not only is our prize collection of these ancient animals, these relics gathered from every corner of the globe, destroyed, but they are now a danger to society as we know it.

You've all seen the reports of the current situation, and the havoc that is being wrought — the animals are everywhere. They roam the streets and go boldly up to people who are going quietly about their business. They confront them and challenge them, and innocent people are put in peril.

The animals are flaunting their freedom in our faces, as if to say we're the ones in the cages now. It almost seems as if they want to share their sort of freedom, but that's ridiculous. We have to stop the animals. We have to lock them up again.

I have been working on the problem of how this can be achieved, and I've come up with the following strategy. It uses tried-and-true principles, but applies them in a new way. It is the reason I have called this press conference today, to release my paper: *The Art of Keeping Animals in Cages Outside the Zoo*. There are five principles.

The first principle is: DIVIDE TO CONQUER.

We have to make different cages and allocate different names. You probably all know that old adage about how a hundred twigs tied in a bunch can't be broken, but how each individual twig can easily be snapped. That's what we must act upon.

Now, we won't call the animals 'animals' any more. We'll call them: Catholic, Protestant, old, young, conservative, radical, high, low, pentecostal, charismatic, apostolic, traditional, mission-oriented, witness, liberation theologist, practitioner of Christian social justice, revolutionary, theologian, born of the Spirit, born of water, baptized once, baptized twice, baptized young, baptized mature. No longer do the animals have one name; they must be divided.

The second principle is: INSTITUTIONALIZE. This is a continuation of the fragmentation process of the first, but this time it is done through imposing an unwieldy, top-heavy, machinery-dominated series of structures. It is easy to do — we just encourage the animals to channel their activities into: committees, constitutions, clubs, fellowships, breakfasts, assemblies, conventions, synods, meetings, thrice-weekly choir practices, quorums, school swimming pools, working bees, buildings buildings buildings, paid preachers preaching only for pay. We have to get their minds away from their ends so that they get lost in their means. That will render them ineffective.

The third principle is: CREATE A CLICHÉ. Let's call the animals things they won't like, things that will make them unattractive to others. Let's pretend that all animals have to be: serious, stern, suited, neat, clean, well-off, middle-class, naive, innocent, dogmatic, unenlightened, teetotal, Bible-bashing. Alternative clichés we could create for them could be: holier-than-thou, hallelujahing, gibberish jabberers, a little sinister, a little too serious and sincere, only interested in money. If we can circulate these clichés widely enough, we'll make the concept of being an animal abhorrent to anyone else, and that will sap the animals' support and quench their spirit.

The fourth principle is: ENCOURAGE TRAITORS. Offer bribes. Use your selling skills. We're producing a catalogue which is just about due off the presses now, that will describe all the bribes available; and let me tell you now, we've got some goodies. Take your pick of the ones you think will serve your purposes best. You can choose from: sex, drugs, friendship, culture, music, food, alcohol, houses, cars, business lunches, retirement packages, power, learning, lotto, hope, gratification, truth, justice, politics, love, life everlasting, and more. We can wrap these little beauties up so that the animals won't have a clue of how to use them; and when they abuse them, the animals will be in big trouble, because we'll be waiting to grab them.

The fifth principle is: COVER UP. Don't encourage the animals, don't let them think that they have anything better than us, anything that we might want if they told us about it. Don't let them see that we're: lonely, sad, disillusioned, battle-wearied, hurt, empty, worried, dissatisfied, hollow, searching, greying, crying, dying. Keep all those things covered up. Lie if you have to. We can't let them see our weaknesses.

These are the five principles to the art of keeping animals in cages outside the zoo. We have to follow them to the letter if we are going to survive this menace. It seems too late to get them back into the zoo, so let's keep them locked up outside.

The animals want to take over our world. It seems they have a vision for it. They want all of us. Don't be fooled. You've been used to staring at them in their cages on Sundays, but all that is past now. This is war. We have to be careful — our whole identity is at stake. Go out there, use my five principles, but be careful. The spirit on their side is powerful — no one knows just how powerful yet — and we have to try to stay out of its reach or . . . or . . . we could end up as animals too.

Spy vs spy

That bloke has got no brains! When they were handing them out, he was off buying a hot dog. Absolutely hopeless! Always sticking his long nose in where it doesn't belong. Always sticking his foot halfway down his throat in his eagerness to show what he knows. I don't know why they keep him on!

And his effort this last time — that was the final straw! I'm going to see the Chief about him, to ask for his removal. And if the Chief won't do that, he'd better at least give him Agent 13's job. If he doesn't, I'll quit. I'm sick and tired of having my cover blown and my operation spoiled. He'll get me killed one of these days.

Take this last effort, for instance. I'll see if I can explain what happened without exploding or having a nervous breakdown.

I was on assignment in the city. I had to choose a public place, settle myself in, and check out what the people were doing. We've been wanting to get some information on what KAOS was doing in public places for a long time. We use it to help us learn what not to do.

I, of course, went undercover. I put on shades, a trenchcoat, a false moustache, and a hat, pulled down low over my eyes. I bought a newspaper with a prominent politician's photo on the front and hid behind it. By cutting the eyes out from the photo, I could survey the scene.

When I was comfortable, I lit a cigarette, then quickly got a fire extinguisher off the wall and put out the fire I caused. I don't think anyone noticed, so all I did was coolly adjust my sunglasses and return to my spying.

All was going well until a group of teenage girls came squealing toward me. I quickly checked my dress, but they said they thought I was from a rock band, and would I give them my autograph? I growled at them and told them to nick off. They spat on my shades, and went.

Night began to fall. It crept up on the city like a cat stalking a mouse. There was a sudden leap, and the city was dark. It was actually a power failure, but it looked very effective — the streets seemed mysterious, and people walked around like shadows, their footsteps muffled. I nearly felt scared, and would have called the Chief on my thong-phone if I'd had twenty cents.

By the time the lights came on, I was perfectly at home, completely undercover, perfectly merged. No one could tell that I was different from all these others. I had succeeded.

And I would have stayed successful too — if it hadn't been for that stupid great bumbling loud-mouthed . . . person!

What does he do? Does he follow the manual, sidle up alongside me, facing the other way, and surreptitiously, through the corner of his mouth, deliver the password? Could he manage anything as terribly difficult as all that? No, of course he couldn't! He has to stroll in, happy as can be, whistling *When the saints go marching in*, our group's badge in broad fluorescent light on his chest, and say in his loudest possible voice: 'G'day! Shalom! How are you?'

Of course, I had palpitations on the spot, but I kept my cool and growled at him to sit down and shut up. Before I could go any further and hiss that I was successfully undercover, ready to spot the minutest of crimes of the opposition, the silly twerp yells to a girl just walking by: 'Hey, sister, do you know Jesus?' — and a stupid great smile on his face as he said it.

What on earth was this irrepressible idiot doing? 'Shut up, will you?' I spat. 'Do you want everyone to know who we are and for whom we're working?'

'Yes', he said.

I don't know how he got through the screening process, but this one was just nuts. He kept going on about how

Property of
A.S.I.O.
P.T.O.

wonderful it was to be on the Lord's side, and how he wanted to tell everyone. I told him I'd 'wonderful' him with a size-9 thong if he didn't shut up. He just kept going on about how he wanted to tell everyone about CENSORED. That was just too much for me.

'Look kid', I said, 'I know you're young and enthusiastic, and you have ideas, but they're no good. People won't listen to you. They'll just laugh at you, or worse. They can't stand us — they want to wipe us out.'

'And it seems like you're willing to let them', he interjected. I could have knocked him into next year for saying that, but I didn't. I tried to be patient.

'You don't know what you're saying. I've been where you're going, and I know what it's like. It's enough of a battle surviving undercover, without coming out into the open like you're doing. You're not only making life difficult for yourself; you're jeopardizing our whole operation. We're trying to fade from view. We don't want people to know we still exist.'

The young bloke got upset then. He yammered on and on about wanting to tell people the Good News that had found him. He didn't want to keep it to himself; he was scared others might miss out. I got stern then.

'Listen here, Sonny. It's all right for you to have your ideals, I can sympathize with that. I used to have ideals too. But I've learnt a bit more about the world since I was as wet behind the ears as you are, and now I'm going to give you a word or two of advice. If you want to survive and enjoy a nice comfortable life, you'll shut up about being a Christian. You'll be a bit pragmatic. You'll play it quiet. Slink into the background. Never be too adventurous. Always hide behind a disguise or three. Never let them know who you really are, or what you really feel — it's the only way.'

He got up then, and began to walk away. He'd only gone a few steps, when he stopped and turned back to look at me. 'Listen', he said, 'if that's how you are, and if that's what the organization is like, I want no part in it. You tell them that. I'll go out on my own and tell whoever I like all the things I know

110

that have changed my life so much. I'm not going to hide the fact that I'm a Christian.' Then he disappeared into the crowd.

'You little fool!' I called after him.

I don't know whether his threat to leave was genuine or not. It'd be easier for everyone if it was. As it is, it's a shame that these young recruits have so much enthusiasm and so little intelligence; they make it hard for all the rest of us. Look at the trouble I got into after that little episode. Some people must have heard us, and they came up and asked me about what being a Christian meant. It was an hour before I could convince them that I didn't know anything, and that I was only a visiting rock star.

Moriarty

Moriarty.

That's the name that's going to be hand-painted on the boot of my wife's Morris Minor.

My wife has always loved Morris Minors. They're those little squat cars that look as if they've only ever been driven by old ladies — and only to church. Their shape resembles a bubble, or an off-colour Volkswagen.

If we're driving anywhere and my wife sees a Morris, she yells: 'Look, Shoog, a Morris!', and I drive off the road and up a tree in fright. She's done it so often that she's even got me doing it now when I'm driving along by myself — which might explain some of the strange looks I get at traffic lights.

If there's ever a Morris on TV, in an ad or a soapie, the cry is: 'Look, Shoog, a film-star Morris!'

One day we saw a Morris exhibition. There was a whole oval-full of Morrises — row after row of the things. They all seemed to be in excellent nick, and there were lots of open bonnets, lots of chrome, and lots of big fat tyres. There were even baby-truck Morrises. Of course, my wife fainted and required a massive burst of mouth-to-mouth resuscitation, but I didn't mind — until a tow-truck driver volunteered to administer it.

We're not rich, and it's enough of a struggle running a 1974 Cortina, without thinking of running another car as well, so my wife was resigned to never getting a Morris. To soothe her disappointment, she got a Morris key-ring, with which she pretended to be happy. I've often caught her staring wistfully at it, stroking it and just dreaming.

And dreaming would have been all that she was able to do, if it hadn't been for the mechanic uncle who told us of a $250 Morris at the wreckers. Naturally, I made a crack about that being the most suitable place for a Morris, but I didn't protest too loudly as we zapped over to take a look.

The Morris was in reasonable condition — it needed a new gearbox, a new bumper, a new rear panel, and a few other bits and pieces, but otherwise it was OK. It wasn't black, but it was very dark green, so it almost was. (Happiness is a *black* Morris Minor, in case you didn't know.)

We couldn't really afford the Morris, but we bought it, anyway. We managed to scrape up enough dollars to cover the cost of the parts we needed, which we got from another wrecker. Now my wife reckons she's going to work pumping petrol so she can get hot-pink lambswool seat covers.

Before we actually bought the Morris, before I put my signature to the cheque that left our bank balance at the grand total of $3.29 (before bank charges and State and Federal taxes), I made sure I asked at least three million people whether we should get the car or not. I suppose, when I asked, there was a certain tone in my voice that said: 'Please say we should get it', but even if there wasn't, all the advice was to get it.

My wife took that advice and put it, with my arm, halfway up my back. I looked at the money in the bank, and wondered if it wasn't safer and more sensible to leave the money there as a security for a rainy day. Then, because I realized how much and for how long my wife had wanted a Morris, and how quiet it would (hopefully) make her, I agreed with her that we should take the risk and get the Morris. And that's the story of the birth of the 1958 Morris that is soon going to have 'Moriarty' painted on its boot.

It doesn't matter what you do in life, there always comes a point where you have to make a decision for yourself. You can get advice from a hundred different sources, you can spend years weighing up the pros and cons, you can check and check and check and check, but finally, you have to make a decision for yourself. And almost always it will involve some risk. Especially when it seems as if we are surrendering one solid form of security for a security that is a bit different.

I suppose that we all feel the most secure when we've got a herd of dollars safely locked away in a bank account, or when we've got a car or house paid off. Or when we're married, so that we can't be lonely any more. Or when we've got a job, so that we can't be unemployed.

It is surprising that, when you've achieved all those things, and when by rights you should have no more insecurities, you suddenly discover some gaps that you hadn't recognized before. There is still loneliness, still fear of the future, still searching for reassurance of your own worth. And all the cheap substitute securities we might try, all end up proving pretty worthless.

It is at this point that you realize that the only true security is to be found in God. Jesus comes right out and says it. He makes the bold offer:
> 'Ask, and you will receive; seek, and you will find; knock, and the door will be opened to you. For everyone who asks will receive, and anyone who seeks will find, and the door will be opened to him who knocks' (Matt. 7:7,8).

That sort of offer sounds like a real bargain. Like a $250 Morris at the wreckers. That doesn't mean the decision is any easier to make. The decision to move from having trust in material things, and the security they offer, to putting your trust in God, is a monster. You can ask people what you should do, you can try to make a rational decision, but, ultimately, you really have to take a risk, take the step in faith.

Jesus describes this step in a parable called 'The Parable of the Hidden Treasure':
> 'The Kingdom of heaven is like this. A man happens to find a treasure hidden in a field. He covers it up again, and is so happy that he goes and sells everything he has, and then goes back and buys that field' (Matt. 13:44).

That's the step of faith Jesus wants us to take.

The next time you're out driving your shiny new car, and you find yourself stuck at 15 km/h behind a dark green 1958 Morris Minor with 'Moriarty' written on its boot, and with a cute little blonde driving, don't swear or toot your horn — wave. Then think of the security Jesus offers you as a result of that step in faith.

The teddy bears' picnic

Every kid has some sort of teddy bear. To love and punch and take to bed.

I had a teddy bear when I was a kid. (I've got a wife now.) My teddy bear wasn't one of those special, all-purpose, fancy-fur, made-in-Japan-or-America type teddy bears. It wasn't operated by batteries or silicon chip (the only chips in those days were the edible ones), and it didn't blink its eyes, rub its tummy, or wet its nappy. It didn't even squeak.

My teddy bear was made out of an old tea-cosy. It was a slightly nauseating shade of yellow, with black paws. The shape of the tea-cosy meant that my bear had a belly that rivalled the best of those on display after four pm on the third day of a Test match down on the Hill or in Bay 13. Its arms and legs were tiny, and its facial features were a couple of buttons for eyes and a bit of wool for nose and mouth.

It wasn't the most handsome teddy bear in the world — but then its owner wasn't the most handsome kid the world had ever seen, either. But I was pretty keen on the old bear. He slept on my pillow alongside me every night, after waiting all day for me to come home, and I never once heard him grunt: 'Where have you been? How come you're so late?' or anything like that.

My brother also had a bear, but his was of the manufactured panda variety. A shrimp of a thing, but very muscular, and done in a dramatically symmetrical black and white.

Unfortunately, our two bears didn't get along. No matter how many truces we called, no matter how lengthy the peace negotiations, my brother and I just couldn't get them to stop fighting and become friends. As soon as we had gone to bed, and the prayers had been said and the lights turned out, the bugle-call to battle would sound.

Because we had double bunks, there were some astonishing manoeuvres. I don't know if you've ever seen a ten pm flying bile-yellow teddy bear double-banger belly-flop-from-the-top-bunk move, but let me assure you that it's an awesome sight.

The bears fought like madmen (madbears?). There were karate chops and head-butts and overhead jujitsu nose-scrunchers, and of course the teddy bear specialty: the teddy hug.

My teddy was big and solid and very enthusiastic. He could take a lot of punishment, but he lacked the stamina to mount much of a counter-attack. After ten minutes he'd be exhausted, and the panda would move in for the kill, using its superior muscle-tone to claim victory.

After the battle, I'd have to collect the pieces of my teddy because he always seemed to lose his head in battle, or a limb or two — in which case he was rendered 'armless. The next day Mum would don her Chief-Surgeon, Doctor-Kildare cap and perform astonishing capitation surgery that even the greatest micro-surgeons wouldn't dream possible.

Poor old teddy had a hard life. Besides the fights, he seemed to have a penchant for leaping into rubbish bins, and I've always had the nasty suspicion that my brother used him to practise his torpedo punts.

Despite all this, and despite my teddy's distinct lack of handsomeness, good taste, and fitness, he remained the best teddy bear in the world. He'd be the one to stand out at a teddy bear's picnic. And he was better than any other toy too — no matter how new or shiny or clever it might be. And I never got sick of him, like I got sick of everything else. If you can call what a kid feels for a teddy bear, love, then I loved that fat old thing. Maybe it was partly *because* he was so bashed up and ordinary-looking that I felt that.

I reckon that's one of the best things about Jesus — the humble way he came to earth. He didn't come as a super-cool royal figure, starring in all the women's magazines. He wasn't decked out in the best that money could buy. He didn't spend all his time with the hoity-toity top-hat-and-tails set of society, sipping wine and munching caviar. That sort of Jesus wouldn't have meant very much to us ordinary people.

Jesus grew up in the household of a carpenter in a scrubby little town. He never had any great piles of money; in fact, it seems as if he never had any. He walked everywhere, in the dust, and he talked to everyone. He was a simple, ordinary bloke.

It is very easy for me to relate to that sort of image of Jesus. In Jesus, I can recognize something of the ordinary person that I am.

Maybe because of that, sometimes we forget to give Jesus the respect we should. He's made a huge effort to be close to us, but maybe sometimes we abuse that, or take it for granted. We should never let the humble appearance fool us; this man is God.

Another thing I've noticed is that, when you're a kid, you're allowed to have a complete love and trust and faith in something like your teddy bear. But as soon as you start to get a bit older, people start telling you to grow up and to leave that sort of kid's stuff behind. They say you have to be mature, that you have to learn to manage by yourself. They say that to be a mature adult you have to do without any crutches.

You'll find that people put Jesus in the same bag. They'll tell you that he's just a crutch, a toy, a security blanket, a childhood fairytale, and that if you want to be grown up you've got to leave all that behind. They say that it was all very nice while it lasted, but that it's irrelevant to life when you're older.

And that might even sound like a sensible, mature sort of argument. What I'd argue is that it is essential that we retain the child's ability to trust completely, to have total faith in, and to love fully. As mature people, we will of course learn more and understand more about God, but we need to keep that childhood innocence, even when people make fun of us for it.

We're lucky. We know God who came to earth in a form with which we can readily identify. Let's have a childlike faith in him, and not get conned into thinking that, because we're grown up, we have to grow out of God. Remember that, the next time you're walking through the woods, tripping over picnicking teddy bears.

The perfect story

The perfect story takes hold of its reader with its first few words and never lets go. It holds its reader in the palm of its hand, and plays games. It tosses the reader in the air, and pretends it is going to let the reader fall and smash into the ground, but at the last second it relents and catches the falling person.

The perfect story knows where it is going. It knows the route ahead and has planned its journey. Detours might beckon, but unless they can help or lead back to the initial route, the perfect story will avoid them.

The perfect story knows all the facts, but it shares only a limited number. It creates its effect by the facts it decides to share. It might be a jealous story, which protects most of its secrets. Or a vicious story, which gives only one side of the situation, so that a particular character gets slandered. Or it might be a playful story, which just teases its reader.

In the perfect story there are shuddering climaxes that send the reader scurrying for a quick coffee and cigarette, and there are moments of absolute calm. There are moments when the reader expects a shuddering climax, but is given only silence.

The reader may finish the perfect story, put it back on the shelf, and walk away. But the perfect story can never be forgotten. It remains.

If any of you know the prescription for a perfect story, perhaps you could drop me a line. We could work out a deal, and I can guarantee that we would both soon be millionaires and on the front covers of literary magazines everywhere. In the prescription you'll need to identify the elements required, their quantities, and any special conditions necessary for their combination into the perfect story.

Let's make a start here, and see if we can identify some of the elements that go into producing a good, tending-to-perfect, story. We'll need a good idea that has enough meat in it to make a substantial casserole of a plot. The plot in turn will need to be clear and logical, at least to the author. We'll need some interesting characters, with enough depth to be human and the ability to make decisions. And then we'll need the basic skills of language: grammar, spelling, vocabulary. The other essential ingredient is a litre or two of liquid paper.

If we can manage to put together all those things, would we then be able to write the perfect sotry? Are they all that is required?

It has been said that if you sat a chimpanzee at a typewriter for a long enough period of time, eventually that chimpanzee would type *Hamlet*. It might take a zillion years, but theoretically it *would* happen.

Consider that for a minute. If the chimpanzee typed an identical *Hamlet*, correct down to the very last comma, pun, and archaic English usage, would you be able to tell the difference between it and the one Shakespeare wrote 400 years ago?

That's a difficult question.

I hold what I suppose is the romantic view, that you would be able to tell the difference. I know that it seems impossible, but I believe that some invisible spirit of the personhood of the author always comes through in a piece of writing. I don't know how, but it is somewhere between the lines. The words might all be the same, but somehow the personality and intent of the author communicates itself, shares its spirit.

It is difficult to describe and define that spirit. It is easy enough to feel when it is present in a particular work of art — a book, a film, a piece of music, or a painting — but just what it is, is a little harder. I think of a piece of music like Handel's *Hallelujah Chorus*, or a film like *Apocalypse Now*, or a book like *The World According to Garp*, or a painting like the *Mona Lisa*. Perhaps I could sit down and draw up a list of all the elements that make these works so good, but I don't think that would help very much in defining the spirit in them that makes them so memorable, alive, and permanent.

Part of the reason for that, I think, is that my personality is somehow involved there, too. It is as if there is some sort of reaction between my personality and that of the creator of the work of art, and that together they produce the aura which makes the piece so special.

As an attempting writer, I try to write so that that reaction can occur. I don't have a formula for it, but I believe that what I have to do is write so that there is space for that reaction to happen. Maybe that is unachievable for me, but it's a goal. If it ever happens, I'll have a perfect story.

God's Word is *the* perfect story.

You might find that a little hard to believe if you've just ploughed through one of the heavier sections of the Old Testament. I must admit that there are times, as I'm reading those sections, when I just have to stop and come up for air. But what makes the Bible *the* perfect story is the fact that the Spirit of God is communicating to us and is giving us space to react.

The Bible is a living story. It hasn't died, but it still pulses away and calls us into it. It invites us to read and partake and participate. We are part of the story. We are the people God is addressing; it is to us that his message is directed. Therefore we are a part of the story's life. It is that reaction between God and us that makes it *the* perfect story.

And while we are on the subject, let's make it clear that, although human beings have penned the actual words we read, it is God who is the real author of the Bible. Therefore it is authoritative and inerrant. And so we can have total confidence in every promise that God makes to us in it. Don't let's forget that.

I'm going to keep writing and keep trying to write the best stories that I can. But, as for perfect stories, there is only one, and I'm going to keep on reading it, over and over again. And why shouldn't I — I've got a starring part.

Off the high diving board

From its cold wet base, the diving board seemed to be very high. Its top was somewhere far off in the heavens. It was enough to scare a young boy into goose-bumps.

It had been decided by my cousin and brother that we had reached that time of our lives where it was necessary to prove our manhood by leaping off the high diving-board. I would have been quite happy had that decision not been made, but long pants beckoned.

We psyched ourselves for that first big jump by making lots of little jumps. I was an expert at the running bomb from the side of the pool. That wasn't frightening at all — except when, instead of scaring the cute little girl I knew by sight (and whom I loved at first sight), I collected the beefy lifesaver doing tricks with Speedos for a collection of fans. *That* was frightening!

After a series of false starts, I eventually became quite proficient on the small diving-board. Actually, I became quite a little show-off, springing up and down, pretending I had a suntan, flexing little biceps, and puffing out a hairless chest. I did brilliant bombs, but I made sure I did them near the side of the pool, so I could get out quickly before someone bombed me.

But practice couldn't last for ever. The decision had been made to make the big leap, so it had to be made. As we gathered at the bottom of the ladder up to the high diving-board, I realized what a good-mannered lot of boys we were. 'After you.' 'No, after you.' 'No, I insist.' We all went up together.

I don't know what it is about heights, but height looking down always feels about 47 times as great as a height looking up. I was ready to call for oxygen. And cold! Our teeth chattered and our knees banged together like hands on tambourines.

After five minutes of nothing, we all clambered down the ladder again — something about having to go to the toilet. That happened three times before we decided enough was enough.

My brother, being the smallest, was forced to go first. He sat down at the end of the board, and we told him to jump. 'I can't', he squeaked.

'Why not?' we asked.

'I'm stuck', he replied. And stuck he was — fear had paralysed him. There was only one merciful thing to do. My cousin did it. A run, a spring, and a bounce, and my brother was free, and hurtling through the air with the greatest of ease.

It was unfortunate that he didn't time his scream better. It only began to leave his mouth as he hit the water, so the bottom heard most of it. We realized his timing was bad when he spluttered up two bucketfuls of chlorinated water after he'd reached the surface.

By the time he'd reached the side of the pool, though, he'd pulled on a brave face, and as he strutted/limped back to the diving-board, he boasted about how easy and what good fun it was. Which meant that my cousin and I had to take the plunge too. We did, enjoyed it, and spent the rest of summer impressing everyone with our blood-curdling leaps.

You have to go off the high diving-board to be a committed Christian. You can spend your whole life sticking to doing the easy things you've always done, or you can put yourself on the line.

It's easier just to be an anonymous face around the church once a month. It's easier not to tell anyone that you're a Christian. It's easier just to roll along, not getting involved, never actually going out of your way to make some commitment to God. But that's the sort of gutless, lukewarm Christianity God condemns.

> 'I know what you have done; I know that you are neither cold nor hot. How I wish you were either one or the

other! But because you are lukewarm, neither hot nor cold, I am going to spit you out of my mouth!' (Rev. 3:15,16).

That's what you call not pulling your punches!

The thing about being a laid-back Christian is that you never give God the chance to show you just how exciting being a Christian can be. You have to accept the challenge and take the leap off the high diving-board.

Sure, it's frightening; and sure, it seems like a huge commitment to make — especially when you're feeling pretty comfortable the way you are. I'ts not strange to have doubts and fears, but the challenge remains. It's the challenge to stand up and shout: 'I'M A CHRISTIAN!' And then to live it.

And just so you don't get the wrong idea, that commitment is not just a once-off thing that, once made, never has to be faced again. You face the challenge every day, day after day. There are always going to be challenges to your faith and to your commitment to Christ; and each time there is, you're going to have to make the decision whether you sneak back down the ladder with your tail between your legs.

In Luke 14:25-33, Jesus talks about what it costs to be a disciple, and he doesn't hide the fact that there is a cost and a step of faith required:

> 'Whoever does not carry his own cross and come after me cannot be my disciple' (v27).

> 'In the same way', concluded Jesus, 'none of you can be my disciple unless he gives up everything he has' (v 33).

That is not an easy option, but it is the option we take if we are serious about following Christ, and if we really want to experience all the blessings of being a Christian that he offers. Maybe the best thing we can do is to ask, as the apostles of Jesus did in Luke 17:5, for Christ to 'make our faith greater'.

'The Lord answered, "If you had faith as big as a mustard seed, you could say to this mulberry tree, 'Pull yourself up by the roots and plant yourself in the sea!' and it would obey you" ' (Luke 17:6).

Let's leave the mulberry tree just for now, and simply ask for the faith to go off the high diving-board into a true and lasting commitment to Christ.

Faith

If you've ever been in a church when the creed has been confessed, you've probably noticed the way people bow their heads, and how their voices descend into a mumble, and how their 'I believe . . .' sounds about as confident as someone predicting an Australian victory over the West Indies at cricket. It's almost as if the people are ashamed of what they're saying, and they're trying to be anonymous so that no one can identify them with what is being said.

I feel really strange sometimes about saying 'I believe' — as if it doesn't go far enough, as if it admits a doubt, as if it acknowledges a possibility that what is being said might not be true.

Football commentators might, in previewing a game, say, after summing up all the evidence: '*I believe* the Magpies will win on Saturday'. There is an equal — and in the case of the Collingwood Magpies that I barrack for, a greater — possibility that they won't. The commentator only believes they will on his interpretation of the available facts.

I once talked to a fairly famous Christian 'talker' about teaching one's children — not that I have any thoughts in that direction at the moment — about God. He said he would tell his children what he believed, then tell them about other religions, then allow them to choose what to believe for themselves.

Now, maybe all the child-rearing experts and so-called enlightened thinkers everywhere are getting on their feet and applauding that as a fine theory, but I reckon it's a load of rubbish.

The way I see it, there is no choice possible. There is only one God. There is only one Christ, and he has done what the Bible tells us he has done. There is no room left for any other god — there *are* no other gods. The God I know is not just the best of a bunch of gods competing in some sort of heavenly

126

Olympics for the laurel wreath of humanity's affection. God is not just the most correct of a number of possibilities. God is God — full stop!

I don't just believe; I know. It's a fact. I can't prove it, but the faith God has given me proves it for me. I can only live and share it as a fact. There is no alternative.

For me, to say that human beings had a choice of gods, and that I merely recommended God as the one that I thought did the best job, would be like strolling out on a bright summer day and saying: 'Well, most people would say today is a bright summer day, but there are some who would say it is snowing, and there are some who would say it is night time. Personally, I *believe* that it is a bright summer day, but you have to make your own decision for yourself' What a lot of rot! The question is just as clear-cut with God.

There is one God, the God of the Bible. There are a heap of tin-pot idols cluttering up the earth, but they are so puny they count for nothing. God is God. I don't just believe that, I *know*. Faith makes that a fact. And I make no apologies.

The fat little man with the big red flag

Just down the road from where I live, there is an intersection that is famous as the worst intersection in the Southern Hemisphere. It has a railway crossing, a pedestrian crossing, twenty lanes of traffic, a fish-and-chips shop, and a fire station.

Because it is practically impossible to avoid this intersection, you have to allow an extra half hour for your journey — that's how long it takes to get through the intersection. No matter how carefully you plan it, how quickly you speed or how slowly you crawl, the light will always be red when you get there.

You might think that all you have to do is wait until it turns green. Wrong! Just when you think the light is about to turn green, when you've already slipped back into gear and released the handbrake, and revved the engine in preparation for a cop-show squealie, a train comes.

I say 'comes', but I don't mean that it passes through the intersection. First the train has to stop at the station just down the track a bit. The railway signals aren't smart enough to know this. They see a train in the distance, say: 'Oh oh, here's a train coming, better flash the lights and lower the booms', and do so. They don't care that the train stops in the station for half an hour while the driver has coffee.

Finally, the train goes, and you think 'At last!', but you've forgotten trains coming from the opposite direction. It is an incredible intersection. Couples are known to have got engaged, married, and to have become grandparents waiting for a green light.

That's the intersection on a normal day. Let me tell you what happened the other day.

I don't know what caused it. Someone probably insulted them, or they decided to go on strike, or there was an internal malfunction, but whatever it was, the booms stayed down and the lights kept flashing. There was no sign of a train. Cars banked up for kilometres in every direction. Paper boys became millionaires. And I got mad.

My fingers drummed on the steering wheel. My lips moved silent curses against a certain intersection, and then against intersections in general. I tooted my horn. I glared at my wife and told her it was her fault.

All of a sudden, one very impatient person did a very brave, and very stupid, thing. He drove around the boom and under the flashing lights. And made it. And was on his way.

Of course, the lights got angrier and flashed even stronger, but you can guess what happened. Soon there was a whole stream of traffic sneaking its way through the intersection. It was a bit of a muddle, but it worked reasonably well, until a train really did come. I've never seen cars move that fast in all my life.

After the train had passed, the lights kept etc, etc. People were too scared to attempt to sneak through now, and it looked as if there would be more hours of waiting. Then, like the Lone Ranger or Superman, to the rescue from out of the blue, there appeared a fat little man with a big red flag.

He contrived to lift the booms up — they work on balance, so that wasn't very hard — and then stood in the middle of the intersection, waved his flag, and directed traffic. The traffic lights were still doing their own thing, and the railway lights were still flashing, but now there was someone to give a guide, someone to follow and obey. You could almost see the ends of the shiny bumper bars turning up in a smile.

I don't know if that fat little man was from the fish-and-chips shop or from the railways. What I do know is that, with his big red flag, he was the most important man in that whole suburb at that moment. He had power, control, and responsibility, and no one had any qualms about following his direction. He was a solution at which people grabbed.

All around us there are people who have problems and who are desperate for solutions. When the problems hurt like loneliness does, or like fear and lost love and insecurity and unemployment and separation do, then people will grab hold of any solution that comes along. They are open to exploitation of the worst kind, and there are any number of cruel and conniving people in this world, willing to move in on them.

And if the hurting people can avoid the exploiters, they still might not get much further than the dead-end alleys of worldly pseudo-solutions. Security might seem to be a steady income, or science and medicine might seem an alternative to death. Sycophantic friends might be bought as a hedge against loneliness. Introversion might be a wall against the harsh reality of the world outside their body.

These are no solution. These are just Satan with his bag of tricks, springing traps for the unwary.

There is only one solution. You can't go past it, and it is deceptively simple.

> 'If you confess that Jesus is Lord and believe that God raised him from death, you will be saved. For it is by our faith that we are put right with God; it is by our confession that we are saved. The scripture says, "Whoever believes in him will not be disappointed" ' (Rom. 10:9-11).

Sitting in that traffic jam at that crummy intersection, watching all those people grabbing hold of the solution that the fat little man with the big red flag offered, I couldn't help but be reminded of the solution God offers. I just wish that people would grab hold of that as easily and firmly and as full of trust. I guess that's my prayer.

A rock'n'roll psalm

Organ music and slow singing are OK. Folky, strummed guitars and sweet harmonies are fine. Negro Gospel spirituals are great. But what I'd really like to hear, just for a change, is a hard and heavy rock'n'roll psalm.

I can't write music , so what I'll write are some words that sound like the noise that is banging in my head. You add your own electric guitars, and wheel out your own massive drum kit.

The psalm goes something like this:
(There's a second of silence; then, from out of the distance comes the beat of a drum.)
In the distance, in the silence, from nowhere
Comes this pain.
It lies waiting, anticipating, the clouds breaking
In my brain.
It grows louder, it grows nearer, ever stronger,
Calling me.
Hear the thunder, pulling under, eyes in wonder
At the murder scene.
(The beat is loud, and it echoes in a solid rhythm, and then it suddenly explodes into a very fast rock'n' roll beat.)
Bright light from a tunnel.
Screaming workmen dream of beer.
Rattle belting along metal.
Pain bleeds from unstopped ears.
No quiet in this killer,
Crushing in this simple skull.
No rest until the morning,
But it's never going to come.
(The drums are joined by bass and thrashing guitar. The song pounds along at a million kilometres per hour.)
Eight hours in the factory,
Eight hours in the pub.
Try and see the family,

Before the day is done.
No hope for the future,
They're going to close down.
Got no super or a pension.
Won't you buy another round?
This isn't a solution,
But why should I stop to care?
It's hard to be committed,
When your future's disappeared.
Cut off the power!
Cut off the lights!
Cut off my manhood!
I'm gone, I'm out of sight!
SCREAM!
(The voice fades away, and the music continues its harsh thrashing song. The guitar moves into a solo that bleeds and then begs. It falls away until it is only a rhythm. That begins to falter. It staggers about drunkenly, before collapsing into a single soft bass beat. It becomes somewhat sterner — you can almost hear nails being bashed into wood. A synthesizer swirls up and cloaks the rhythm with gloom, and a strange and mechanical voice from out of a tunnel intones.)
We are the dead men.
Captured in cloud and stone.
We are the dead men.
We're cold.
We are the dead men.
Caught still before our time.
We are the dead men.
Don't leave us alone.
(The synthesizer swirl swings higher into an angelic realm, and children's voices sing.)
Gloria — in excelsis.
Gloria — today.
Gloria — no more waiting.
Gloria Deo.
(Their chorus is repeated until it is a chant, and the synthesizer fades away to nothing. It is replaced by a tortured lead guitar coming from the distance but getting nearer and nearer. It gets louder and sweeter, louder and sweeter, until it is only a couple of simple notes being repeated, quicker and quicker. It breaks back into the same rock'n'roll beat as the second part of the psalm, and the same voice sings.)

Bright light from a graveyard.
An empty tomb.
A woman weeping,
But she's not alone.
A voice she remembers
Calls out her name.
A smile as she recognizes,
Things aren't ever ever ever ever going to be the same.
*(The music is climactic. Through it can be heard the
voices of a man and a woman talking, laughing, crying.
The music goes as high as it can go, then gradually
winds down into the same simple drum beat that
occurred at the beginning of the psalm. The same voice
sings.)*
From the distance, from the silence, from before,
Came this man.
From the clouds, he took hold of my breathing,
Made me a man.
Gave me laughter, held me close, made me stronger;
I'll never be alone.
Hear the thunder, hear the sound of your name,
    open your eyes to wonder.
Things will never ever ever ever be the same.
*(As the music slows and softens toward silence, a kind
voice is heard speaking, saying:)*
For God so loved the world, that he gave his only Son.

And that would be the end of my rock'n'roll psalm. Unplug
the amps, and let's go home.

Twenty tongue-twisters to try twisting your tongue around

Twenty tongue-twisters to try twisting your tongue around? That's a bit of an exaggeration for the sake of the effect — there's really only a couple, and they're a little later on, so you'll just have to wait a bit before you set your tongue to work.

When I was at primary school, it seemed that nearly every one of my teachers got a wonderful kick out of giving us students tongue-twisters to try to say. They'd watch us screwing our little faces into knots, concentrating really hard so that the words that came from our mouths would make sense, and then they'd laugh happily when we failed.

I don't know whether all my primary school teachers were kinky, or just thought that straining little children's tongues was an acceptable educational practice. All I know is that when Peter Piper picked a peck of pickled peppers, he did so without my help. When I tried it, a pickled piper pecked a pep of peppled peters.

It was even worse when Tammy, the young lady who had caught my attentions in an unbelievable crush, said sweetly and sincerely: 'How much wood could a woodchuck chuck if a woodchuck could chuck wood?'

'What's a woodchuck?' I replied, thick-headedly.

I couldn't work out why I got such a withering glare until Mean Pete, my crew-cut arch-rival for Tammy's affections, said, very clearly and very correctly, and with his puny little chest thrust out as far as it would possibly go: 'How much wood could a woodchuck chuck if a woodchuck could chuck wood? Why, that's easy — any bird-brain knows that! As much wood as a woodchuck could chuck if a woodchuck could chuck wood.' As he spoke the last chuck, I realized that the one true love of my tenth year of life had passed for ever from my grasp.

TONGUE
Twisters

With all this talk of tongue-twisters, I reckon it's about time you too had a chance to make a fool of yourself. Here are a couple for you to try — not real difficult, just a couple fairly basic limbering up exercises. Try saying each of them about four times, quickly, and I'll meet you when you're finished.

> 1. The notion of devotions floating on the ocean with a motion like a lotion is a notion without devotion to the laws of locomotion for lotions floating on the ocean.

> 2. The toffy cockie coughed softly for coffee to unblock the toffee he'd recently scoffed. But the cocky tough whose toffee he'd scoffed, scoffed the cockie's coffee, then knocked off his block.

Dear, dear, dear! What's that tangle I see protruding from your mouth? Couldn't quite manage it, hey? Well, you be quiet now, give your tongue a rest, and just sit back and listen.

Did you know that the Bible contains a tricky tongue-twister? It is difficult to say, and looks even harder to decipher. It was written by St Paul:

> 'I know that good does not live in me — that is, in my human nature. For even though the desire to do good is in me, I am not able to do it. I don't do the good I want to do; instead, I do the evil that I do not want to do. If I do what I don't want to do, this means that I am no longer the one who does it; instead, it is the sin that lives in me' (Rom. 7:18-20).

The tangle that your tongue gets in trying to say all that, and the confusion that arises when you try to work out what it means, both reflect the tangle and confusion people get into when they encounter the phenomenon in life that Paul is talking about. If we look closer, we can see that Paul is writing about something we all often feel.

When a person becomes a Christian, his (or her) life changes. No longer does he want to flit about doing just whatever he pleases, without any regard for whom he might be hurting. Instead, Christians want to do good. It is their way of responding to the love that they recognize God has given them.

It is relatively easy to want to do good — most people think they want to do good. But actually to *do* good is another cake of soap. Doing good costs. It means sacrifices. It means going out of your way. It means dropping *me* from the number-one spot. That's not easy. In fact, let's be honest about it, that's really hard. In fact, it's pretty well impossible. So, while we might *want* to do good, most of the time we don't manage to do it.

Paul's right on the football there — he recognizes at least that part of us. He goes on to say that 'I do the evil that I do not want to do'. He's been spying, I reckon. How many times haven't you done things about which, immediately you've done them, you think: 'O, what sort of klutzmeyer am I? Why on early warning systems did I do that?' That's the power of sin: It makes us do what we don't want to do. Sure, we can try to fight it; but sin is powerful, and it usually ends up making our efforts look pretty pathetic.

Paul explains about this in his next sentence. He says that when we do what we don't want to do, it's not we who are doing it, but sin. It's sin that's stopping us from doing the good that we want to do, and making us do the evil that we don't want to do.

All right, we've wormed our way out of that tongue-twisting situation, but aren't we still in a bit of a tangle? It's sin that is to blame, but how do we get rid of it? If we're still caught in sin, we're guilty.

Listen to what Paul goes on to say a bit later on:
> 'There is no condemnation now for those who live in union with Christ Jesus. For the law of the Spirit, which brings us life in union with Christ Jesus, has set me free from the law of sin and death' (Rom. 8:1,2).

That's our reassurance. When our whole life is a tangle, when we're utterly frustrated by our inability to do the good that we want to do, and to stop doing the evil that we don't want to do, then we need only look back to the promise that there is no condemnation for us if we 'live in union with Christ Jesus'.

Now, get out the back and practise those tongue-twisters! I want them word-perfect the next time I see you.

My Sociology essay

Sociology is one of those subjects you do if you happen to have trendy leftie politics in your system. It is also one of those subjects you do if you can't think of what else to do. I won't tell you which category I fall into.

In Sociology, theoretically it doesn't matter what your politics are, provided you can set out clear and coherent arguments for your position. (It should be noted that the arguments that appear clear and coherent to everyone else do not necessarily appear so to a very Marxist, very ivory-tower, intellectual, student-of-the-sixties lecturer.)

And, in Sociology, if you can use a thousand big words to every two small ones, then you are well on the road to brilliance and a high mark in the 5,000-word essay that you have to complete by an impossibly-short deadline.

In case you haven't guessed by now (in which case I would be tempted to ask whether *you* were a Sociology student), I have just finished work on a Sociology essay. My topic was 'The Rise of the New Right (a conservative political grouping) in Australia'. Pretty thrilling, don't you reckon?

What makes it even more thrilling is that there have to be 5,000 words of it. 5,000 words is about 20 double-spaced typed pages. Which is a heck of a lot for my two typing fingers to handle.

My essay is cross-referenced, bibliographed, introduced, concluded, quote-and anecdote-containing, in places italicized, and utterly resplendent in the subtle autumn tonings of spilt coffee and liquid paper. It is also page-numbered, photocopied, stapled, and handed in.

You will, of course, realize that before the actual typing happened there were preliminary drafts. And research.

138

(Research = two million hours in a library, reading obscure articles by dead people in defunct magazines, photocopying the same for future reference, taking notes in lectures, and panicking.)

Thankfully, now it is all finished. I have made the deadline, and, presumably, have no more worries. Wrong! It is now that all the *real* worries start.

I try to wait patiently for the essay to be marked. I try not to gnaw my fingernails to the bone, or to pull out all my hair. I try to remain calm until my Sociology lecturer has finished adulterating my paper with his red biro, distributing question marks and exclamation marks and rude remarks with gay abandon. I try, but I fail, and I don't stop trembling until I've seen that final mark, the most important mark —my percentage mark.

I could pretend that I was confident of passing. I could rest easy in the assurance that I had done lots of work and tried very hard to do my best. I could believe that my attitude had been good, and that I had been enthusiastic — at least until the 47th typing error on the first page. Surely I deserve to pass — even if it is only out of pity!

But, alas, my lecturer takes none of that into account. All he looks at are those words I've tried so hard to arrange for maximum effect. There lie my prospects for the future, for success or failure. There are no second chances.

I am very glad that my Sociology lecturer isn't God (although he often seems to think he is). More correctly, I am very glad that God doesn't judge me like my Sociology lecturer does. That is, on the basis of my performance in a test. If God did, I'd fail miserably.

Look at some of the areas in which I'd blow it. How many times have I forgotten the needs of my brother or sister? How easily haven't I fallen into the habit of trusting myself rather than God? How many times have I used God only as a convenience or as a last resort? How many times have I sinned?

How correct, then, is Paul's summary of my situation:
> 'Everyone has sinned and is far away from God's saving presence' (Rom. 3:23)!

If God sat in heaven with a big black book, marking down all my sins, errors, and mistakes, the book would fill in a moment, and I would fail.

There is an old joke that says that in heaven there is a clock for every person on earth; the hand on this clock moves one second every time that person sins. The punchline of the joke is that they're using my clock in the office for a fan.

We fall far short. If that were the way things remained, our situation would be hopeless — we would be lost and condemned. Like Martin Luther before he rediscovered the Good News, we would be locked up in depression. There is no way that we can make ourselves fit for heaven by ourselves.

So thank God that we have the Good News:
> 'But by the free gift of God's grace all are put right with him through Christ Jesus, who sets them free. God offered him so that by his death he should become the means by which people's sins are forgiven through their faith in him' (Rom. 3:24,25).

From being utterly unworthy, I am made worthy to live with God. That is an incredible transformation, and we on earth cannot fully comprehend its magnitude. It's like my Sociology lecturer telling a tutor to completely fix up my Sociology essay so that it could get full marks. Actually, I suppose, it is like telling the tutor to write the essay for me.

Let's thank God that he doesn't ask us to pass a test on our own merits. No matter how hard we tried, we would fail. Instead, he has given us the 'free gift' of his grace, and that's a gift no one can afford to knock back.

Carte blanche *for SYIs*

She was about twenty. Dressed in tights, ankle boots, and a bold pink polka-dot shirt. Wore heavy earrings and heavy make-up. She was a Serious Young Intellectual. You'd call her pretty if it weren't such a sexist thing to do.

She said this was her trendy punk look. Well, maybe it was. It fitted well in our Poetry Writing class. Well, it fitted into the trendy younger half, the neatest collection of SYIs you're ever likely to find. The other half of the group were older, and older-fashioned. And I was in the centre, doing a hot-coal quickstep between one and the other.

Anyway, she pulled out her poem like John Wayne going for his gun in one of those old Westerns, and let fire. This was not her usual melodramatic self-indulgence. It wasn't her 'Im-a-poor-depressed-young-person-writing-great-poetry-about-all-the-things-that-make-me-such-a-wonderfully-interesting-poor-depressed-young-person' type of poem, but something much more bitter. It was a volley of accusations against Christianity, which she called 'Two thousand years of a lie'. Very over-the-top!

When asked what had motivated the poem, the girl replied that she had recently decided to leave religion behind her and become the person she thought she was, and that the poem expressed what she felt about that decision.

There was a burst of applause from the SYIs hunched smoking about the room. One motivated young chap, who is for ever marching against things, stood up and called: 'Congratulations'. A major celebration ensued — it was like a reverse baptism.

When you're being a quiet-in-the-corner Christian, that sort of thing gives you a bit of a shock. I had never realized that SYIs were so actively anti-Christian. I knew they regarded Christians as silly, old-fashioned, unenlightened wimps, but I didn't realize they felt this strongly. I thought they were apathetic; I didn't know they were bitter.

There have been other times, before I could stop myself, that I have made challenges, based on my Christian principles, to the current thinking of a class. Now, anyone with any brains knows that it doesn't exactly help one's popularity or reputation to attack the consensus reached by SYIs. To do so because of Christian principles is lunacy; and I admit here and now that I'm not the fearless confident Christian I could be. But there have been times when I've made a challenge, and each time the bitterness of the reaction has surprised me. I am used to the feigned boredom and cynicism of SYIs, but this reaction was new. It was obvious they felt threatened.

In an academic institution, you find a lot of people thoroughly opposed to any concept of God. They've crunched their way through enough books to convince themselves that they don't need God, and that, therefore, God does not exist. Graffitied on one of the walls at the college I attend was the line: 'God is dead. — Nietzsche' (Nietzsche was a German philosopher who went crazy). Some very smart person had written underneath: 'Nietzsche is dead. — God'.

I don't know where SYIs get their image of God from. From the way they talk, anyone would think that God was some sort of brutal taskmaster who existed only so that he could spend his time prying into people's lives, making sure they had no fun, and checking that every time they did something wrong, they got punished.

They see the church as an arm, an extension, of this type of God. They see it as an instrument that exists only to make people feel bad and guilty about themselves and their bodies, and to put the people of earth into one of two boxes: the sinners, and the saints.

They think that being a Christian means never having fun, never thinking, and never sinning. If they catch a Christian doing something wrong, they point a finger and say: 'There! I told you so. All Christians are hypocrites.'

From what I know of SYIs, the things they want in life are sex (smorgasbord-style), alcohol (by the barrel), and whatever other drug it takes to keep them from thinking about what their bodies are doing. Because God, and the church

142

proclaiming God's Word, won't give them a *carte blanche* to do whatever they want, the SYIs reject him. And get drunk and laid.

If you watch the atheistic intellectuals on TV, or read their columns in papers, you'll soon see that they aren't really concerned about much more than their own pleasure. It seems that this is the only reson they have for ignoring and rejecting God.

I don't know where this sort of people get their information from — maybe 'religion' has got to take some blame here — but the God they're talking about isn't anything like the one I know, the God of the Bible.

God enables Christians to be the happiest — in fact, the only truly happy — people on earth. This comes from the simple fact that Christians are saved for a perfect life with God. Secondly, they have the freedom to enjoy all of God's gifts in the most pleasure-giving way — in moderation.

God gives us alcohol, not to get drunk on, but to enjoy. God gives us sex, not to play with irresponsibly like a toy, but to enable us to come to the fullest and happiest relationship with the person to whom we've pledged our lives. God does not prohibit pleasure; he sets guidelines wherein it can serve us best.

Frankly, I get very tired of all these cynical and bitter SYIs, and their greed for a *carte blanche* to do whatever they want. I think their narrow-mindedness is evident in the way they spend half their lives blaming religion and God for the problems of this world, and the other half trying to hide their pathetic insecurities in a haze of sex and booze and intellectualism. Their inability to listen to anyone with a different view from theirs, and the way they rest on preconceived notions without attempting to discover the truth about the subjects on which they pass judgment, show their pettiness very clearly.

There are a lot of SYIs in the world, and they're constantly going to try to club you over the head with their particular brand of serious young intellectual atheism. Don't take any nonsense from them, but look at them closely and check out the life they're living. You'll soon see that SYIs can't be taken seriously.

You got to grin

Car clagged out today. Died noisily. I got it to the overalled monkey, before its last breath, in fits and starts and stops.

Monkey let out a long low whistle: Three days' work.

Couldn't afford a train home. Couldn't afford a telephone word. Had to hitch. Face long. Not real happy.

A lot of cars sped past my outstretched thumb. Sped past smirking. New and shiny, and thinking of stories of hitch-hikers raping and robbing and beating. Sped past. My legs aching, thumb wilting. Long way home.

Old blue rust-bucket pulls up in front. Holden. Guy inside young, brown hair, long and curly. A mo. An earring. 'Yeah. Get in'.

Said he was unemployed. Six months now. Got retrenched so two seventeen-year-olds could get their first job — part of some Government scheme, two for the price of one. He wouldn't have cared — young kids need jobs or they go crazy. 'I used to be crazy' — except he'd worked hard, never complained, on time, for four years.

The dole is seventy-something bucks. Not a lot to live on, if you're living alone. So, after nine years from home, has to go home, to Mum and Dad — tail between the legs — and try to find a home in the small bedroom at the end of the hall. Between the dog and the just-about-paid-off-mortgage.

Told me he'd once been in the army, training to be a medic. Wanted to help people. Not enough certificates to play doctor. Put up with the life, with shifting every six months away from mates. Put up till someone let slip that army qualifications meant nothing in the world outside khaki. A young man's dream goes spinning.

But he said you got to grin and bear it. So he grinned and bore it. Quit the green machine and found a new job and set

144

up a place. Went to night school to get qualified. Went well until someone nicked the car with all the books.

Kept grinning and kept the job. Things looked toward good. Some money. A personal loan from big kindly brother bank for a stereo. Wonderful sound. Until it gets nicked, too. Twenty bucks a month for twenty years for nothing. And now the job's gone too.

It's a great life, he said.

Why didn't you blow your brains out? I said.

Thought about it, he said. Then, you got to grin and bear it. And he stopped the car and let me off outside my house. He wasn't going this far, but he'd seen this guy hitch-hiking along the road, tail between the legs, and he knew all about shiny cars and tail between the legs. And he knew how to grin and bear it, and he could see that here was someone who needed to be shown how to grin and bear it. So he went my way.

You tell me a sad story, I'll tell you one sadder.

You say you got a heart that's breaking, I'll show you one that's shattered.

You say you lost love, I say you ain't been looking.

You say you're hungry, I point to your belly.

You say, God, this world hates me, God says, I love you.

You say you got nothing left to say, I say, about time.

Take a look at you, pal, take a look at what you been given. And what you still got coming. You got it all, friend. You got no right to go round, tail between your legs, thinking, I got nothing, ain't my life sad?, the whole world's bad and against me.

Person, you got to get down on your polished knees, and you got to close your eyes and think. Then open them and grin. Yeah, grin. Cos you got a God come already, come and bore it all. For you. Bore it all up there on that old tree. And you got nothing now worth worrying about, cos you got it all.

Go out along the highway. Pick up a hitch-hiker, tail between legs. Say why you're grinning. Shout why you're grinning. And keep grinning. You got to grin.

The axe-murderer

It was just a little after midnight when the girl got into her car. It was a long drive down through the mountains to her home in the suburbs, and she was a little tired. She turned on the radio, and turned it up loud — she liked music in the car at night.

The girl had been driving only a few minutes when she noticed the headlights of a car behind her. As it got closer, the girl steered to the left-hand edge of the road so that the car could pass. It started to, then dropped back in behind. The girl could see no reason why.

The car stayed very close behind the girl, and it made her nervous. She accelerated to put some distance between her and it, but the car behind accelerated too. Then its lights flashed on to high beam. The girl wondered what was wrong, but then dismissed it as just the result of a bump in the road.

The girl turned the radio up louder, and concentrated harder on the road ahead. The car behind flashed its lights again. The girl knew that it was deliberate, and she began to feel a little worried. She decided to see whether the car really was following her, and turned off into a road that was darker, windier, lonelier. The car behind seemed to get even closer, and its lights flashed continuously.

A real fear was growing in the girl's belly, now. She knew where she was, but her confidence was disappearing. To make matters worse, the needle on the petrol gauge had moved inexplicably quickly toward EMPTY. Fear was becoming panic, and the girl's driving started to suffer. She was speeding now, wandering all over the road and screeching around corners. The car behind stayed close, so the girl decided to make an all-out dash for home.

It took only a few minutes to reach her street, but to the girl it seemed like for ever. She sped down it, skidded into her driveway, leaped from the car, ran inside, and locked the door. As she slid shut the last bolt, she heard the car pulling up in her driveway. It stayed there, its lights still on.

The girl dialled the emergency number for police. The voice at the end of the line said that there was a car in the area and that it would be there in a few minutes. The girl hung up the phone and looked through the curtains at the front window of her house. The lights of the car behind hers dazzled. She trembled.

In a moment, there was the sound of a speeding car. It slammed to a halt in front of the house, and two armed policemen jumped out. They went up to the car behind the girl's, and in burly police fashion ordered the driver out. He was an elderly, balding man. The police said they were placing him under arrest. The man replied: 'Don't arrest me. Get the guy with the axe in the back of the girl's car.' One of the policemen went to the girl's car, where he found a wild-haired man nursing an ugly axe.

Apparently, the elderly man had seen the silhouette of the man with the axe, as he had gone to pass the girl's car. He had followed her to try and warn her.

That story is true.

It is possible that we might feel that we spend a lot of our lives being followed and threatened by God. It might seem that, wherever we turn, however hard we try, we can't get away. He might always seem to be close behind us, some vague anonymous sort of enemy, a kill-joy, a threat to what we might think is our right to an earthly kind of security. Maybe we feel that all God does is peer over our shoulder and say: 'Hey, stop it! That's wrong. That's no good for you'.

And if we feel like that, maybe we try everything we can to get away from God. To leave him far away in the distance. Turn up the sound of a plastic world, speed as fast as money can take us, steer a wild way through the darkest paths of existence. But whenever we turn, he's still there. There's no escape; the threat, the danger remains.

Like the girl in the car, we're not recognizing the real danger. It is not God that is the threat to our freedom, and happiness, and security. God is warning us of the danger that has wormed its way much closer to us, so close that we can't see it. It is the danger that creeps up on us, that offers us a whole lot of 'good' things at no cost, that tries to persuade us that our real friend is an enemy.

This is the danger of not knowing God, or knowing him but ignoring him. It is Satan playing his devilish little tricks, his sleight-of-hand games, his fast-talking confidence tricks. He has only one purpose in mind — and that is to separate us from God. He doesn't want us to know the strength and protection that God offers. He doesn't want us to grow into the people God gives us the potential to be. Satan just wants us for himself, to toy with as he likes, to murder at his pleasure.

It can be easy to get confused, to think the enemy is a friend, and the friend an enemy. We can be like the girl in the car. The shattering realization of how close the real enemy can get should be enough to make us cling as closely as possible to the friend who is there to warn us and to protect us.

As Peter says:
> 'Be alert, be on the watch! Your enemy, the Devil, roams round like a roaring lion, looking for someone to devour. Be firm in your faith and resist him, because you know that your fellow-believers in all the world are going through the same kind of sufferings' (1 Peter 5:8,9).

Me old blue ball

I have just finished writing 2,000 words about the part Phronesis plays in Aristotle's account of the moral life. My brain is somewhat exhausted, and the two fingers I use for typing are but a tattered remnant of the fine digits they once used to be.

When I get to this state, I like to go outside and do something wildly physical. It so happens that the sun is shining and the sky is blue. A man would have to be an idiot to stay inside.

I get out me old blue ball. *My* old blue ball — sorry. The ball used to be the shape and size of a basketball. It now resembles an off-colour egg — after a nasty collision with a barbed-wire fence. However, it is still kickable.

So I kick it.

I am no George Best or Pele (the only famous soccer players I know), but I enjoy booting the ball in a fashion that approximates soccer.

There is a toolshed out the back that makes a good target, and occasionally I hit it. Very occasionally. A lot of the time I spend playing soccer is spent climbing over the neighbour's fence to retrieve the 'ball-burster' that went astray. Or persuading the other neighbour's vicious Corgi that a blue rubber ball would not make a very good lunch; it agrees, and goes for an ankle instead. At still other times I get trapped inside giant prickly man-eating bushes, while trying to rescue the ball held securely in the highest branches.

Of course, when the ball is not in problem areas like these, playing with it is great. I dextrously dribble past the fledgling orange tree, bluster brilliantly by the bird-applauded barbecue, and skilfully side-step a pile of canine fertilizer. Then I let fly with a tremendous shot for goal.

Sometimes when I shoot for goal, I wind up on my backside counting clouds. At other times, I kick big-rock-containing

grass and break numerous bones. Then there are the times I don't kick anything at all.

In case you think me absolutely hopeless, let me assure you that I do sometimes kick goals. If I kick one goal, I'm likely to get a run on, to hit a hot streak. I'll shoot ten out of ten. I'll dob them in from impossible angles, around corners, over my head — I won't even need to concentrate. I flash and feint and wave to the crowd, and then suddenly remember, with a crash, that there isn't enough room for me to run under the clothes line.

When this happens, and after I have regained consciousness, I make a few between-the-teeth comments about the parentage of that ungrateful wretch of a blue ball that has so thoughtlessly led me into a confrontation it should have realized I had no chance of winning. The ball replies suitably coolly, and tells me to stop being a cissy and to get up and keep playing. I do.

I aim for the goal and hit a geranium. I aim at the clothes line for revenge and hit a Cortina. Then I tell myself I was really aiming for the Cortina and only pretending to aim for the clothes line in order to psyche out my opposition, which I have undoubtedly succeeded in doing.

And I reassure myself that even if I didn't actually get the goal, I got very close, and it doesn't really matter because the target is very small and far too hard for any normal person to go even close to getting. So I have actually done very well, and am probably the best player on the ground.

I aim once more. The ball leaves my foot at the correct angle. It swerves through the air beautifully, on target for the centre of the goal. It will be the best goal of the day, and will be replayed in slow motion at least a thousand times. I picture the glory . . .

. . . As it is about to score, from nowhere there leaps a goalkeeper with the agility of a cat. He knocks the ball harmlessly wide.

Living as a Christian is like playing backyard soccer with a beat-up old blue ball.

I love a sunburnt stomach

> I love a sunburnt stomach,
> A nose of blistered pain,
> Legs that are raw and peeling,
> And back a bright pink plain.

Australia is lovingly called the sunburnt country. That's nice. Its people, however, are meant to be sun-*bronzed*. That's a big difference.

My skin is white. I'm not ashamed of that. I only worry when I wear shorts. If I stand too long in the same place, people start trying to kick footballs between my legs. That is embarrassing.

Every year, on the first day of December, I sit down and ask myself whether this year I will attempt a tan. Will I lie in the sun for hours on end, clothed in nothing more than tight and tiny Speedos, or will I wrap myself up in light, loose-fitting clothes?

If I decide to attempt a tan, I attempt it very carefully. I make good friends with a tube or two of zinc cream, and I make sure I never expose myself to the sun for too long. Well, that is my plan, but it rarely works out that way. The sun has a nasty habit of making me drowsy.

Never fall asleep in the sun!

I fell asleep in the sun once. When I woke, I was roasted. Underneath my left nipple was a white hand-print from the hand I had forgotten to remove. The rest of me was the sort of red that nuns warn young girls about.

To ease the pain, I stepped into a cold shower. That is to say, I only turned on cold water. Steam billowed out of the shower as if the water was boiling. It was me that was boiling.

It is when you are in a shower that you discover in how many different places the human body can get sunburnt. Like under the armpits, between the toes, on the head where the part in the hair is — all those tender, normally unexposed areas. They hurt the worst.

There are many remedies for sunburn. None of them work. You can spend thousands buying out the chemist shop, or you can try one of the home-cures that have been handed down from the early settlers.

'Cold tea', says one grandmother.

'A mixture of vinegar and baby oil', says another.

'Peanut butter and honey', says a third.

Nothing works!

Usually, someone in pain gets a lot of sympathy. The sunburn-sufferer doesn't. The sunburn-sufferer is told: 'It's your own fault — I told you not to lie in the sun so long. It serves you right.' That sort of comment is really encouraging to the victim writhing in agony in a bath of molasses!

After the initial stinging has passed, the itching begins. It's always worst in that one spot in the middle of your back that you can't reach.

Finally, the itching passes away, and you start to think that it was all worthwhile because it looks like you're going to be left with the start of a tan. Ha! Big joke! You've forgotten peeling. It begins about a week after the initial catastrophe. You discover a lot of friends then, because everyone likes to peel off someone else's skin. They have contests to see who can get the biggest slab, or who can clear a given area in the quickest time. The whole process gets under my skin.

No one in any of the ads on TV or in the magazines gets sunburnt — they're all sun-bronzed. That is, they look sun-bronzed. What has really happened is that they've been painted with a fast-drying acrylic mixture. Nevertheless, there are so many of these sun-bronzed Aussies that you feel as if you can't step outside your front door unless you're sun-bronzed too.

This can lead to some ridiculous situations. I had a friend who went to Bali, where she hoped she'd get a suntan. Before she went, however, she had to go to the solarium, to get a suntan so that she wouldn't be embarrassed when she was getting a suntan.

Other people plaster fake tanning-gunk all over themselves, leaving white spots where they couldn't reach and splotches where they spilt the stuff, and ending up with hands that look like they've been used for walking on for a week. Rich people eat bowls of tablets that are supposed to tan them from the inside out, but only manage to turn them an interesting pleurisy-yellow.

You'll notice, too, that nobody ever mentions what a suntan now does to skin later on. It's not polite to talk about cracked, chapped, and wrinkled leather in the vicinity of beautiful brown bodies. And it is absolutely wrong to even breathe a hint about skin cancer.

That's the trouble with so many things in this mixed-up, shook-up world. They get held up as wonderfully good and fantastically desirable. We're told that they are the things we should spend our lives working toward, aiming for, getting. We're supposed to feel guilty if we aren't.

What never gets talked about are the problems these things cause: the immediate pain of false priorities that put people last on a long list of things to be thought about, and the longer-term pain of separation from God, which ultimately means extinction and punishment.

Let's just look at a couple of examples: free sex, and maximum money. Both money and sex are good for us if used properly; but look what happens if they get held up as the number-one goals of life, the things that must be possessed at the cost of everything else.

In the area of free sex, a lot of people get hurt, emotionally and physically. The results are broken homes, broken hearts, and broken bodies. In the area of maximum money, we get corruption, greed, crime, and violence. And those are just the immediate consequences.

154

The longer-term pain is the wedge that things like unrestrained sex and lust for money can drive between a person and God. They cause a separation that leads to the person's eternal death. Things become gods, and they replace the only God with the power to love and save.

I don't know if St John ever got sunburnt, but when he concludes his first letter he makes some points similar to those I've been groping toward:

> 'We know that we belong to God even though the whole world is under the rule of the Evil One. We know that the Son of God has come and has given us understanding, so that we know the true God. We live in union with the true God — in union with his Son Jesus Christ. This is the true God, and this is eternal life. My children, keep yourselves safe from false gods!' (1 John 5:19-21).

Think about that this summer, as you're lying in the harsh Australian sun getting your own sunburnt stomach.

Iwaserefirst God
I Was
ere
Krause

After

Well, you made it, did you? Congratulations. (Or are you one of those who skips the middle of a book and goes to the end to find out who the murderer was? If you are, then beware — the butler will get you too!)

I feel pretty exhausted, having finally made it to here, and a bit stripped bare. That's mostly me that you've seen running around the pages, and it's a bit embarrassing to have to admit to that.

But I suppose it's much better that you see me as the fairly ordinary, fairly klutzy person that I am, than get a picture of me as some sort of perfectomundo Christian, qualified to give advice left, right, and between the big ones.

Being, or becoming, a Christian doesn't mean you suddenly become perfect. It doesn't mean that you immediately stop feeling sexual desire, or that your taste for a good beer dries up. It doesn't mean that you are transformed from Joe (or Josephine) Cool to Claude (or Maude) Wimp. What it means is that you come to realize who and what you are, and how much you need God. You accept God, and the gifts he offers — in particular, Jesus Christ. In response to God's goodness to you, you make an effort to do what he wants. You blow it about a million times, because you're still human; but God's there, waiting, ready to forgive.

Being a Christian enables you to put things back into perspective. Maybe you still can't help worrying about computers running your life, and bombs dropping on your head, and your footy team getting the wobbles in the finals. Maybe you still get lonely, and depressed, and scared about dying. Those things happen; but being a Christian lets you thrust all that on to God. If we can learn to do that, it leaves us free to explore and develop the person each one of us is. We can begin fulfilling our potential. That is exciting, and that is giving glory to God for the life he has given us — the life we begin on earth, the life which we continue for ever in heaven with him.

If you feel as if someone you know might enjoy, or be helped by, this book, give it to them. (I should really tell you to go out and buy a dozen copies, but this wasn't written for the money.) And if you feel like writing to me to tell me what you thought, then do it. I'd appreciate it.

There's nothing much else to say here, so I'll just finish off with the blessing Paul used to close his second letter to the Corinthians:

> 'The grace of the Lord Jesus Christ, the love of God, and the fellowship of the Holy Spirit be with you all' (2 Cor. 13:13).

Seeya!